SLOW C
BEST NEW

SLOW COOKING: BEST NEW RECIPES

Annette Yates and Norma Miller

RIGHT WAY

Constable & Robinson Ltd
3 The Lanchesters
162 Fulham Palace Road
London W6 9ER
www.constablerobinson.com

Originally published in the UK 2006 under the title
Fresh Ideas For Your Slow Cooker

This fully revised new edition published by Right Way,
an imprint of Constable & Robinson, 2009

Copyright © Constable & Robinson 2009

A copy of the British Library Cataloguing in Publication Data is available from the British Library

ISBN: 978-0-7160-2222-0

Printed and bound in the EU

CONTENTS

CHAPTER		PAGE
Introduction		7
Quick-Check Recipe Index		9
1.	Hints & Tips	13
2.	Lazy Breakfasts	17
3.	Slow Soups	31
4.	Families Unwind	47
5.	Relax with Friends	67
6.	Just You & Me?	83
7.	Strictly Vegetarian	99
8.	Perfect Pasta, Rice & Grains	119
9.	Hot & Spicy, Easy Peasy!	135
10.	Leisurely Puds	153
11.	Cool Cakes	173
12.	Top Preserves	187
13.	Clever Extras	197
Index		201

INTRODUCTION

Slow cooking is in vogue. Tender and succulent joints of meat and the rich, subtle flavours of slow-cooked dishes are again in favour. An appetising prospect, certainly, but how can you achieve these results in your own kitchen? With busy modern lifestyles, most of us just cannot manage to have food roasting, braising or simmering all day long in the oven or on the hob. The solution to this conundrum is your slow cooker. This economical and versatile machine can be trusted to produce wonderful, traditional and innovative meals, ready just when you want them, while you go out and about doing other things.

Using fresh and store-cupboard ingredients, lots of exciting spices and aromatic herbs, our fully-tested and foolproof recipes are designed to obtain the maximum benefit from your slow cooker. Starting with our lazy breakfasts, there are ideas for dishes throughout the day and for every day: high days and holidays, weekdays and weekends alike. There are small-scale meals for one or two, and dishes for large parties, family or friends. Plenty of serving suggestions and hints and tips accompany the recipes.

You can travel the world with your slow cooker. After all, slow cooking is the time-honoured foundation to many of the finest global cuisines. You can create surprises too. Just look at our section on cakes. And you can slow-cook rice, pasta and grains as well. When you do have all day to prepare for a large gathering, and your oven and hob are fully utilised, your slow cooker can add significantly to your capacity for catering on a grand scale. And don't forget how energy saving your slow cooker is, when compared with the cost of producing equally sumptuous fare by conventional means.

By bringing slow cooking up to date and combining the traditional and contemporary, we can all have the dishes we most want to eat, dishes for where and who we are.

QUICK-CHECK RECIPE INDEX

1 hour
Chocolate & Rum Fondue, page 164, + 30 minutes
Hot Cracked Wheat & Ham Salad, page 132, + 15 minutes
Rice with Smoked Haddock, page 24, + 30 minutes

1–1½ hours
Brown Rice with Leeks, Bacon & Cheese, page 126
Warm Figs with Orange, Honey & Walnuts, page 23

1–2 hours
Mushroom & Parmesan Rice, page 124
Warm Millet Salad, page 134

1–3 hours
Bagna Cauda, page 80
Two-Cheese Fondue with Crispy Bacon, page 70

1½–2½ hours
Chocolate & Lime Pancakes, page 20
Courgette & Mushroom Frittata, page 26
Devilled Frankfurters, Gammon & Smoked Sausage, page 28
Extra Chocolaty Chocolate Cake, page 174, + 15 minutes
Seafood in a Wine & Herb Soup, page 84
Sticky Pineapple & Cinnamon Cake, page 182

2–3 hours
Brioche, Banana & Cranberry Pudding, page 156
Egg Custard with Lime & Maple Syrup, page 171
Salmon & Prawns with Vermouth, page 86
Spanish-Style Rice with Chicken, Mussels & Prawns, page 78
Trout & Fennel Pasta, page 121

2–4 hours
Duck with Pomegranate Juice, page 90, + 15 minutes
Greengages with Coconut, page 172
Marrow with Bulgur Wheat, Pepper & Ginger Stuffing, page 112
Pecan-Filled Apples, page 154
Peppers with Spiced Cheese Stuffing, page 88
Plums & Berry Crumble, page 155

2½–3 hours
Chilli Chocolate Sauce, page 194, + 30 minutes
Lemon Drizzle Polenta Cake, page 184

2½–3½ hours
Creamy Squash & Sweet Potato Casserole, page 114, + 30 minutes
Lamb Couscous, page 128
Squash & Raisin Pudding, page 162
Tropical Fruit Pudding, page 160

3–4 hours
Cardamom & Ginger Cake with Sesame & Pine Nuts, page 178
Chilli Brown Rice with Prawns & Seeds, page 125
Chocolate Cake with a Nut Topping, page 176
Citrus Curd, page 192
Sticky Oat, Orange & Walnut Cake, page 180

3–4½ hours
Chocolate Ginger Pudding, page 158

3–5 hours
Chicken Dhal, page 146
Chilli Beef & Chorizo, page 147
Chinese Pork with Cashews, page 150
Mild Lamb Curry with Coconut, page 152
Oriental Chicken with Egg Noodles, page 122, + 10 minutes
Plum Pudding, page 168, + 45 minutes
Spiced Beetroots & Red Cabbage with Tofu, page 104, + 15–20 minutes

3½–4½ hours
Sticky Butterscotch Pudding, page 166

4–6 hours
Aubergines, Potatoes & Carrots with Lemon Myrtle, page 117
Barley Pilaff with Lamb & Mushrooms, page 130, + 1–1½ hours
Beef & Pork Meat Loaf, page 54

Biryani, page 138
Chicken & Prawns, page 68
Chilli Chicken Bowl, page 144, + 10–15 minutes
Chocolate Rice Pudding, page 170
Date & Apricot Relish, page 188
Game Terrine, page 76
"Hunter's" Chicken, page 50
Lamb Chops on Caramelised Squash, page 92
Lamb Meatballs in Tomato Sauce, page 60
Mustard Chicken with Whisky & Wild Mushrooms, page 98
Pheasant in Orange & Apple Sauce, page 96
Quorn Cassoulet, page 108, + 1 hour
Red Pepper Chutney, page 191
Slow-Cooked Gammon, page 66
Thai Green Chicken & Vegetable Curry, page 142

5–7 hours
Green Lentil & Apple Soup, page 44, + 30 minutes
Vegetable Chilli with Pan-Fried Tofu, page 106

5–8 hours
Apple, Plum & Walnut Chutney, page 190
Pasta, Mushroom & Bean Medley, page 120, + 30 minutes
Sweet & Sour Pork, page 64

6–8 hours
Chicken Chowder, page 36
Chilli Venison with Chocolate, page 81
Curried Turkey & Sweet Potato Layer, page 52
Fennel & Red Pepper Soup with Tamarind & Mint, page 43
Flageolet & Black-Eyed Beans with Pistou, page 100
Lentils, Root Vegetables, Star Anise & Lemon, page 116
Potato, Leek & Smoked Ham Soup with Olives, page 42
Root Vegetables & Red Beans in Spiced Coconut Sauce, page 102
Spiced Lamb with Apricots, page 148
Spiced Leg of Pork Cooked in Cider, page 72
Stuffed Shoulder of Lamb with Onion & Courgette Sauce, page 74
Thai Curry Soup with Pork, Chilli & Lemon Grass, page 40
Tomato, Basil & Rice Soup, page 32, + 20–30 minutes

6–9 hours
Leg of Lamb with Red Wine & Lentils, page 58

6–10 hours
Breakfast Fruit, page 19

7–10 hours
Borlotti Bean Soup with Spicy Sausage, page 38
Sweet Potato & Chickpea Soup, page 34
Weekend Porridge, page 18

8–10 hours
Autumn Fruit Spread, page 189, + 5–8 hours
Beef with Red Wine, Garlic & Thyme, page 56
Chickpeas with Cumin, Green Chillies & Parsley, page 140
Honeyed Chicken, page 48
Hot Muesli with Cranberries & Blueberries, page 22
Lancashire Lamb Shanks, page 94
Minestrone Stew, page 110
Tarka Dhal, page 136
Traditional Baked Beans with Pork, page 62

1

HINTS & TIPS

This section is all about how to get the best from your slow cooker and from our recipes

- Just like most kitchen appliances, slow cookers are likely to vary from model to model. Always be guided by your manufacturer's instructions. In particular, check their recommendation for the minimum and maximum quantity of food, and preheating.

- You will need to get a feel of the cooking times too – when you first try out recipes in this book, compare the cooking times with similar ones in your manufacturer's instruction book. You may find you need to adjust our timings slightly to suit your slow cooker. If your slow cooker has only one setting (i.e. it cannot be switched to High, Medium or Low) you may need to shorten cooking times in this book by between 30 minutes and one hour.

- The cooking time on High is generally just under half that on Low. To shorten the cooking time of a recipe cooked on Low (perhaps on a day when you arrive home early and want to speed things up), switch the slow cooker to High setting and halve the remaining time.

- When adapting conventional recipes for the slow cooker, reduce the quantity of liquid by about half and use these cooking times as an approximate guide:

Conventional	In the Slow Cooker		
	Low	High	Auto
½ hour	6–8 hours	3–4 hours	5–7 hours
½–1 hour	8–10 hours	5–6 hours	6–8 hours
1–3 hours	10–12 hours	7–8 hours	8–10 hours

- To encourage even cooking of ingredients, cut them into even-size pieces.

- Remember – meat cooks more quickly than vegetables, so cut it into small dice or thin slices.

- Always thaw frozen foods before putting them in the slow cooker.

- Browning meat and vegetables on the hob before adding them to the slow cooker will usually give a better colour and flavour to soups, stews and casseroles.

- Dried beans and whole peas (and some whole lentils) often need an overnight soak in plenty of cold water before boiling rapidly for 10 minutes, draining and adding to the slow cooker. Red kidney beans **must always** be boiled rapidly for 10 minutes. Always check the packet instructions.

- Rice? Easy-cook varieties usually produce the best results.

- Season only sparingly until the dish is cooked – flavours tend to concentrate in the slow cooker and you may find you need less salt, for example, than normal.

- Some quick-cooking ingredients are best added towards the end of cooking, such as rice, pasta and grains, and vegetables that you want to stay crisp or retain their bright colour. Others, like cream or milk, are likely to separate if added more than 30 minutes before the end of cooking.

- By all means lift the lid to check or stir occasionally. Each time you do, remember to add about 15 minutes to the cooking time to compensate for the loss of heat.

The Recipes

- For convenience, the ingredients are listed in the order in which they are used. Though they are given in imperial as well as metric, you will find the metric measurements easier to use.

- Most of the recipes can be doubled to make extra servings.

- Sometimes you may want to cook a small quantity of food in a large slow cooker. Simply follow the method in the recipe and transfer the prepared ingredients to an ovenproof dish that will fit comfortably inside the slow cooker. Cover the dish securely with foil and add boiling water to come half-way up its sides. Cover the slow cooker with the lid and cook as normal.

- The recipes include basic store cupboard ingredients, including the occasional stock cube and, our favourite, vegetable bouillon powder. Because it's granular, you can spoon out as little as you like.

- All spoon measures are level unless otherwise stated.

- One or two recipes may contain partly cooked eggs – please remember that it is advisable to avoid eating these if you are pregnant, elderly, very young or sick.

- Sometimes we use a stick blender for whizzing soups into chunky or smooth blends (alternatively you could use a food processor).

- Some recipes contain fresh chillies. Do take care when preparing them and remember to wash your hands thoroughly afterwards. Better still, wear rubber gloves while handling them.

- We usually suggest preheating the slow cooker before using, but do check with your manufacturer's instructions to see if this is strictly necessary for your model.

15

2

LAZY BREAKFASTS

Is this your morning to relax and take it easy? After a busy working week or a late night entertaining, with guests staying over, breakfast needs to be there when you want it and hassle-free. Your slow cooker gives you this freedom and flexibility, and the food, when cooked, will stay hot.

About half of the recipes in this section can be left to cook overnight and will be ready when you are for breakfast. The rest can be started in the morning and are ideal for a late breakfast going on brunch. So there will be time for you, your family and your guests to read the newspapers, take the dog for a walk or even go to the gym.

For feeding large numbers, some of these recipes can easily be doubled in quantity.

Weekend Porridge

This porridge, with whole oats, lightly spiced, and with added fruit and seeds, is lovely on a cold winter morning. To make it plain, simply omit the spices, fruit and seeds.

Serves 6–8   *LOW 7–10 hours*

175g/6 oz large rolled oats
1 tsp mixed spice
4 tbsp raisins
2 tbsp seeds, such as sunflower and pumpkin, plus extra for serving
Clear honey, soft brown sugar or demerara sugar, to serve
Milk or single cream, to serve

1.   Preheat the slow cooker on High while you prepare the ingredients. Put the kettle on to boil.

2.   Put the oats into the slow cooker and add the mixed spice, raisins and seeds. Pour over 1.3 litres/2¼ pints hot water (from the kettle) and stir well.

3.   Cover with the lid and cook on Low for 7–10 hours, by which time the oats should be very tender and the porridge will have thickened. Stir well.

4.   Ladle into bowls and drizzle with clear honey or sprinkle with brown or demerara sugar and a little milk or cream spooned over the top of each serving. Sprinkle with extra seeds if wished.

Breakfast Fruit

We prefer to cook the fruit one day and chill it overnight, ready for spooning over hot porridge (see previous page) the next morning. If preferred, it can of course be eaten warm from the slow cooker. We like it for dessert too, with thick yogurt or vanilla ice cream.

Serves 8   *LOW 6–10 hours*

**500g/1 lb 2 oz mixed dried fruit, such as apples,
   apricots, figs, peaches and prunes
Small handful of raisins or sultanas
3 whole cloves or a good pinch of dried ground cloves
1 cinnamon stick
300ml/½ pint orange juice
3 tbsp thin-cut orange marmalade
½ lemon**

1.   Put all the dried fruit into the slow cooker and add the cloves and cinnamon stick. Stir in the orange juice, marmalade and 1 litre/1¾ pints cold water. Make sure the fruit is pushed down under the surface of the liquid (apple rings tend to float so you may need to put them at the bottom and weigh them down with other fruit).

2.   Cut the lemon into thin slices and float them on top of the liquid.

3.   Cover with the lid and cook on Low for 6–10 hours.

4.   Stir gently before serving.

Chocolate & Lime Pancakes

Wickedly tempting, definitely not for a day when you are counting calories. Basic pancakes can be made ahead; they also freeze well, but can now be found in many stores. Wonderful with maple syrup for brunch, or cut into small portions and serve with scoops of vanilla ice cream or even custard for dinner.

Serves 6–8   HIGH 1½–2½ hours

Butter, for greasing
1 lime
8 tbsp nutty chocolate spread
200g/7 oz light cream cheese
6 ready-made pancakes
Maple syrup, to serve

1. Preheat the slow cooker on High while you prepare the ingredients.

2. Lightly grease and line the base of a deep 18cm/7 inch ovenproof dish with non-stick baking paper. (Check the dish fits inside your slow cooker.) Lightly grease another disc of non-stick baking paper for the top. Put the kettle on to boil.

3.   Finely grate the rind from half the lime. Cut the lime in half and squeeze out the juice (about 2 tbsp).

4.   Spoon the nutty chocolate spread into a bowl and stir in the cream cheese, lime rind and juice.

5.   Spread some of the chocolate filling over five of the pancakes, taking it almost to the edges. Layer the topped pancakes in the prepared dish; the edges will curl a little up the sides of the dish. Top with the remaining pancake and gently press the paper disc on top, buttered side down.

6.   Cover the dish tightly with foil and put into the slow cooker. Pour in sufficient hot water to come half-way up the sides of the dish. Cover with the lid and cook on High for 1½–2½ hours until hot.

7.   Lift out of the slow cooker, remove the foil and paper disc and loosen the edges with a knife. Turn onto a warm plate, cut into wedges and pour over maple syrup.

Hot Muesli with Cranberries & Blueberries

A hot mix of cereals, grains and fruits. Don't reserve just for breakfast. A healthy bowl of muesli is good any time of the day and can also be eaten cold. Serve with milk or yogurt. Put in a container and take for lunch. For extra crunch, scatter over a handful of chopped walnuts.

Serves 6–8   *LOW 8–10 hours*

70g/2½ oz whole oat grains
50g/1¾ oz millet seeds
50g/1¾ oz wheat or barley flakes
40g/1½ oz sultanas
40g/1½ oz dried blueberries
40g/1½ oz dried cranberries
½ tsp ground cinnamon

1.   Put all the ingredients into the slow cooker.

2.   Pour over 1 litre/1¾ pints cold water and stir well.

3.   Cover with the lid and cook on Low for 8–10 hours until the grains are soft and the dried fruits are soft and beginning to collapse.

4.   Stir gently before serving.

Warm Figs with Orange, Honey & Walnuts

To serve this taste of the Mediterranean as a dessert, try adding a splash of sweet sherry or Italian Vin Santo with the orange juice in step 3 and then accompany the warm figs with mascarpone cheese, whipped double cream or vanilla ice cream. Any left over can be chilled and served later.

Serves 4–6   *HIGH 1–1½ hours*

8 large fresh ripe figs
Butter for greasing
100g/3½ oz walnut pieces
3 tbsp clear honey, plus extra to serve
100ml/3½ fl oz orange juice
Thick Greek yogurt, to serve

1. Trim the stalks off the figs and cut each one into quarters without cutting all the way through the base. Gently squeeze the bottom of each fruit to open it out, flower like.

2. Lightly butter the inside of the slow cooker. Arrange the figs, upright and in a single layer, in it.

3. Roughly chop the walnuts and stir them with the honey. Put a small spoonful of the mixture into the centre of each fruit. Drizzle the orange juice over the figs.

4. Cover with the lid and cook on High for 1–1½ hours until the figs are soft and warmed through.

5. Carefully lift out into a serving dish and spoon the juices over the top. Serve with a generous spoonful of Greek yogurt and, if liked, extra honey drizzled over the top.

Rice with Smoked Haddock

Based on the traditional breakfast dish called Kedgeree, this also makes a great supper dish. For the best flavour use non-dyed haddock.

Serves 6   *HIGH 1 hour + 30 minutes*

1 medium onion
250g/9 oz easy-cook basmati or easy-cook long grain
  rice
3 medium eggs
About 500g/1 lb 2 oz smoked haddock
85g/3 oz butter
2 tsp fish or vegetable bouillon powder
Small handful of parsley
1 lemon
Salt and freshly milled pepper

1. Preheat the slow cooker on High.

2. Finely chop the onion. Wash and drain the rice. Wrap
    each egg individually in foil. Wrap the smoked haddock
    securely in foil, cutting it into manageable-size pieces if
    necessary and arranging it in an even layer.

3. Heat the butter in a saucepan on the hob and add the
    onion. Cook over medium heat for about 8 minutes,
    stirring occasionally, until softened and just beginning
    to turn golden brown.

4. Stir the rice into the onion, and then add 700ml/1¼ pints water and the bouillon powder. Bring just to the boil, stir well and pour the mixture into the slow cooker.

5. Push the foil-wrapped eggs into the rice and lay the parcel of fish on top.

6. Cover with the lid and cook on High for 1 hour.

7. Lift out the four foil packets and put to one side. Gently stir the rice, replace the lid and continue cooking for a further 30 minutes until the rice has absorbed the liquid.

8. Meanwhile, flake the fish, removing all skin and bones but reserving any juices. Unwrap the eggs, remove their shells and chop or cut into slices or wedges. Finely chop the parsley. Cut the lemon into wedges.

9. Just before serving, stir the fish and its juices into the rice and add the parsley and seasoning to taste.

10. Top the rice with the egg slices/wedges and serve with lemon wedges for squeezing over.

Courgette & Mushroom Frittata

Firmer than an omelette, frittatas are delicious hot or cold and would make a good picnic dish. Serve with hot toast or salad.

Serves 4   *HIGH 1½–2½ hours*

25g/1 oz butter plus small piece for greasing
2 shallots
1 garlic clove
1 medium courgette
100g/3½ oz button mushrooms
8 medium eggs
2 tbsp milk
1 tsp pepper sauce (optional)
2 tbsp fresh thyme leaves
Freshly milled salt and black pepper
2 tsp olive oil

1. Preheat the slow cooker on High while you prepare the ingredients.

2. Lightly grease and line the base of an 18cm/7 inch deep ovenproof dish with non-stick baking paper. (Check the dish fits inside your slow cooker.) Put the kettle on to boil.

3. Finely chop the shallots and garlic. Finely grate the courgette and thinly slice the mushrooms. Break the eggs into a bowl and stir in the milk, pepper sauce (if using), thyme leaves and a little seasoning.

4. Heat the butter and oil in a pan and fry the shallots and garlic for 5 minutes until softened. Stir in the courgette and mushrooms and cook for a further 5 minutes.

5. Remove from the heat, stir in the egg mixture and tip into the prepared dish.

6. Put the dish into the slow cooker. Pour in sufficient hot water to come half-way up the sides of the dish. Cover with the lid and cook on High for 1½–2½ hours until set and cooked through.

7. Lift the dish out of the slow cooker and loosen the edges with a knife. Turn onto a warm plate, cut into wedges and serve hot or cold.

Devilled Frankfurters, Gammon & Smoked Sausage

Hot and spicy, certainly a wake-you-up dish for the morning. Cayenne pepper is hot, so measure carefully. Serve with lots of hot buttered toast.

Serves 6–8   *HIGH 1½–2½ hours*

1 medium red onion
400g/14 oz button mushrooms
400g/14 oz cherry tomatoes
8 frankfurter sausages
250g/9 oz smoked sausage
250g/9 oz smoked gammon
1 tbsp olive oil
2 tbsp Worcestershire sauce
3 tbsp wholegrain mustard
½ tsp cayenne pepper
1 tbsp chicken bouillon powder
Freshly milled black pepper
Chopped fresh parsley, to serve

1.   Preheat the slow cooker on High while you prepare the ingredients.

2.   Put the kettle on to boil. Finely chop the onion. Slice the mushrooms and tomatoes in half. Cut each frankfurter into three, slice the smoked sausage and dice the gammon.

3.   Heat a large non-stick pan, add the sausages and gammon and fry for a few minutes until lightly browned. Transfer to the slow cooker.

4.   If necessary add a little of the oil to the pan and heat. Add the onion and cook for 5 minutes until softened. Stir in the Worcestershire sauce, mustard, cayenne, bouillon powder and a little seasoning. Pour over 300ml/½ pint hot water and bring just to the boil. Stir in the mushrooms and tomatoes and tip over the meat in the slow cooker.

5.   Cover with the lid and cook on High for 1½–2½ hours until piping hot and cooked through. Serve sprinkled with a generous amount of parsley.

3

SLOW SOUPS

Diverse and delicious, all these soup recipes are perfect for your slow cooker. You will find here soups for every day and soups for smart occasions, soups as starters and some that are ideal as main courses. Some soups are chunky and others, after whizzing them with your hand-held stick blender, will produce a silkier, smoother result.

Slow cooking gives soups an extra dimension. The ingredients gently interact, producing complex and satisfying flavours which will delight the taste buds as well as being wholesome and nutritious fare. And there are always those last-minute additions to each bowl as it is served – some crusty bread, a handful of olives, a swirl of cream or yogurt or a handful of fresh herbs.

Tomato, Basil & Rice Soup

Add the rice of your choice – brown, basmati or wild rice are all good. For a lighter soup, perhaps to serve as a starter, simply omit the rice and serve the soup with crisp-fried croûtons.

Serves 6   *LOW 6–8 hours + 20–30 minutes*

1 large red onion
2 garlic cloves
500g/1 lb 2 oz fresh ripe tomatoes
400g can whole plum tomatoes
1 tbsp sugar
1 tbsp tomato purée
Salt and freshly milled pepper
1 chicken stock cube
1 generous tsp vegetable bouillon powder
Generous handful of fresh basil leaves
250g packet of ready-cooked rice
Extra virgin olive oil, to serve

1. Preheat the slow cooker on High while you prepare the ingredients.

2. Put the kettle on to boil. Finely chop the onion and garlic. Roughly chop the fresh tomatoes.

3. Put the onion, garlic and fresh tomatoes into the slow cooker. Add the can of tomatoes, chopping them roughly as you tip them in, and the sugar, tomato purée and a little seasoning.

4. Dissolve the stock cube and bouillon powder in 1.2 litres/2 pints boiling water (from the kettle) and pour into the slow cooker.

5. Cover with the lid and cook on Low for 6–8 hours.

6. About 30 minutes before serving, add the basil leaves and, with a hand-held stick blender, whizz until very smooth. Adjust the seasoning to taste and stir in the rice.

7. Replace the lid and continue cooking on Low for 20–30 minutes.

8. Ladle into warmed bowls and drizzle each serving with a little olive oil.

Sweet Potato & Chickpea Soup

This fat-free soup couldn't be easier to make. If you like spicy flavours, use a hot mango chutney. We like to serve this soup fairly chunky but you can blend it until smooth if you wish (see step 6).

Serves 6   LOW 7–10 hours

2 sweet potatoes, total weight about 600g/1 lb 5 oz
1 potato, about 175g/6 oz
1 red onion
1 medium carrot
1 garlic clove
410g can chickpeas in water
1 chicken stock cube
1 generous tsp vegetable bouillon powder
2 tbsp mango chutney
Salt and freshly milled black pepper
Small handful of fresh coriander leaves (optional)

1. Preheat the slow cooker on High while you prepare the ingredients.

2. Put the kettle on to boil. Chop the sweet potatoes and potato into small pieces. Finely chop the onion, carrot and garlic.

3. Put all the chopped vegetables into the slow cooker. Add the chickpeas, including their water.

4. Dissolve the stock cube and bouillon powder in 1.2 litres/2 pints boiling water (from the kettle) and stir into the slow cooker.

5. Cover with the lid and cook on Low for 7–10 hours.

6. Add the mango chutney and, with a hand-held stick blender, whizz to a thick (but not entirely smooth – see note above) texture.

7. Season to taste and serve with coriander leaves scattered over, if using.

Chicken Chowder

A thick, rich, chunky mixture based on the famous American soup. Serve with hot, crusty bread.

Serves 6   *LOW 6–8 hours*

4 boneless, skinless chicken thighs
2 boneless, skinless chicken breasts
1 large onion
1 large potato
1 large carrot
4 celery sticks
1 tbsp olive oil
25g/1 oz butter
2 chicken stock cubes
1 generous tsp vegetable bouillon powder
1 small green pepper
175g can sweetcorn kernels
Salt and freshly milled pepper
150ml/¼ pint double cream

1. Preheat the slow cooker on High while you prepare the ingredients.

2. Trim and cut the chicken into small pieces. Chop the onion, potato, carrot and celery into fairly small pieces.

3. Heat the oil and butter in a large saucepan on the hob. Add the onion, potato, carrot and celery and cook over medium-high heat for 5–8 minutes, stirring occasionally, until beginning to soften.

4. Stir the chicken into the vegetables and cook quickly for 2–3 minutes until the contents of the pan just begin to turn golden brown. Add the stock cubes and bouillon powder and stir in 1.2 litres/2 pints water. Bring just to the boil and tip the mixture into the slow cooker.

5. Cover with the lid and cook on Low for 6–8 hours until the vegetables and chicken are very tender.

6. Meanwhile, halve the green pepper, remove and discard the seeds and stalk, and slice thinly. Drain the sweetcorn.

7. About 30 minutes before serving, add the green pepper and sweetcorn, adjust the seasoning to taste, and stir in the cream. Replace the lid and continue cooking on Low for 20–30 minutes.

Borlotti Bean Soup with Spicy Sausage

You will need to soak the dried beans overnight before cooking. Alternatively, use two or three 400g cans of beans, drained and added in step 3. For a vegetarian version, add extra vegetable bouillon powder in place of the chicken stock cube and serve the soup topped with grated cheese instead of the sausage.

Serves 6   *LOW 7–10 hours*

250g/9 oz dried borlotti beans
1 onion
1 carrot
2 celery sticks
2 garlic cloves
1 tbsp olive oil
400g can chopped tomatoes
1 chicken stock cube
1 generous tsp vegetable bouillon powder
Salt and freshly milled black pepper
About 150g/5½ oz spicy sausage, such as chorizo
Crusty bread, to serve

1. Soak the borlotti beans in plenty of cold water for at least 8 hours or overnight. Next day, drain the beans and put into a large saucepan on the hob. Cover well with water and boil rapidly for 10 minutes.

2. Preheat the slow cooker on High while you prepare the rest of the ingredients.

3. Drain the boiled beans and put them into the slow cooker. Finely chop the onion, carrot, celery and garlic.

4. Put the chopped vegetables into a large saucepan with the oil and cook over medium heat for 5–10 minutes until slightly softened and beginning to turn golden brown. Add the tomatoes, chicken stock cube, bouillon powder and 1.5 litres/2¾ pints water. Bring just to the boil and tip over the beans in the slow cooker.

5. Cover with the lid and cook on Low for 7–10 hours until the beans are tender.

6. Season to taste with salt and pepper.

7. Cut the sausage into thin slices and divide between warmed serving bowls. Ladle the soup over the top and serve with crusty bread.

Thai Curry Soup with Pork, Chilli & Lemon Grass

Full of oriental flavours this soup is mildly hot. For a hotter version use a few of the chilli seeds. Lemon grass is a traditional flavour in Thai cooking. It looks rather like a dry spring onion – available fresh, dry or in jars.

Serves 4–6   *LOW 6–8 hours*

6 spring onions
1 garlic clove
1 stem lemon grass
Small piece of fresh root ginger
1 red chilli (see page 15)
150g/5½ oz minced lean pork
1 tbsp green Thai curry paste
150ml/¼ pint coconut milk
1 tbsp lime juice
2 tbsp chicken bouillon powder
Freshly milled black pepper
4 tbsp freshly chopped coriander

1.   Preheat the slow cooker on High while you prepare the ingredients.

2.   Put the kettle on to boil. Finely slice the spring onions and crush the garlic. Cut the lemon grass vertically in half. Coarsely grate the root ginger. Cut the chilli in half, remove and discard the seeds and stalk, and finely chop.

3.   Heat a wide non-stick pan, and when hot tip in the minced pork and cook for about 5 minutes until lightly brown, stirring and breaking up the meat with a wooden spoon. Add the spring onions, garlic, lemon grass, ginger and chilli and cook for a further 2–3 minutes.

4.   Stir in the curry paste, coconut milk, lime juice, bouillon powder and a little seasoning. Pour over 1 litre/1¾ pints boiling water. Heat until bubbles begin to rise to the surface. Pour into the slow cooker.

5.   Cover with the lid and cook on Low for 6–8 hours. Stir in the coriander just before serving

Potato, Leek & Smoked Ham Soup with Olives

A substantial soup which definitely could be eaten as a main meal. Do use smoked ham if possible; it adds its own distinctive flavour.

Serves 4–6   *LOW 6–8 hours*

2 leeks
1 large onion
1 or 2 potatoes, weighing about 350g/12 oz
200g/7 oz smoked ham
8 stoned black olives
1 tsp olive oil
2 tbsp vegetable bouillon powder
3 tbsp wholegrain mustard
Freshly milled salt and black pepper
Crusty brown bread, to serve

1. Preheat the slow cooker on High while you prepare the ingredients.

2. Put the kettle on to boil. Thinly slice the leeks and finely chop the onion. Leave the potato skins on and finely chop. Cut the ham into small dice. Quarter the olives.

3. Heat the oil in a large pan and fry the leeks and onion for about 3 minutes until softened. Add the potatoes and cook for a further 5 minutes until lightly browned.

4. Stir the ham, bouillon powder, mustard and a little seasoning into the pan and pour over 1 litre/1¾ pints boiling water. Bring just to the boil and pour into the slow cooker.

5. Cover with the lid and cook on Low for 6–8 hours. Use a potato masher to partially crush the vegetables. Stir in the olive quarters and serve with crusty brown bread.

Fennel & Red Pepper Soup with Tamarind & Mint

Tamarind is a date-like fruit growing in pods. This sour-and-sweet pulp (available as a paste) is so versatile for adding its concentrated flavour to full-bodied dishes. Here it complements the aniseed flavour of fennel and peppers.

Serves 4–6   *LOW 6–8 hours*

2 medium fennel bulbs
2 red peppers
4 spring onions
1 garlic clove
1 litre/1¾ pints vegetable stock
1 tsp lemon oil
1 tbsp lemon juice
1 tbsp tamarind paste
Handful of mint sprigs

1. Preheat the slow cooker on High while you prepare the ingredients.

2. Trim the fennel bulbs and finely chop. Cut the peppers in half, remove and discard their seeds and stalks, and slice thinly. Chop the spring onions and crush the garlic.

3. Put all the ingredients into the slow cooker and stir thoroughly.

4. Cover with the lid and cook on Low for 6–8 hours until the vegetables are tender and soft.

Green Lentil & Apple Soup

Green lentils don't require soaking before they are cooked. For a smooth soup whizz until smooth with a stick blender before you add the spinach leaves. The recipe makes a generous quantity, so could be a main meal.

Serves 4–6   *LOW 5–7 hours + 30 minutes*

200g/7 oz green Puy lentils
1 large red onion
1 garlic clove
3 green eating apples
100g/3½ oz young spinach leaves
1 tbsp olive oil
1 tbsp vegetable bouillon powder
4 sage leaves
1 bay leaf
Freshly milled salt and black pepper
Hot pitta breads, to serve

1. Preheat the slow cooker on High while you prepare the ingredients.

2. Put the kettle on to boil. Wash the lentils in plenty of cold water and drain. Finely chop the onion and garlic. Quarter the apples, remove and discard the cores, and cut into small pieces. Wash the spinach leaves.

3. Heat the oil in a large pan and fry the chopped onion and garlic for about 3 minutes. Add the chopped apples and cook for a further 2–3 minutes until lightly browned.

4. Stir the drained lentils, bouillon powder, sage leaves and bay leaf into the pan and pour over 1.5 litres/2¾ pints boiling water. Bring just to the boil and pour into the slow cooker.

5. Cover with the lid and cook on Low for 5–7 hours until the lentils are cooked and soft.

6. Remove the lid and with a slotted spoon lift out the bay leaf. Use a stick blender to whizz the soup smooth and season if necessary. Stir in the spinach leaves, cover again with the lid and cook for a further 30 minutes. Stir and serve with hot pitta breads.

4

FAMILIES UNWIND

Once upon a time, families used to sit down together to share their main meal of the day. For many of us, this is still an ideal, but how often does it actually happen? For all sorts of reasons (shift work, school, clubs, gym, French classes) we resort instead to hurriedly prepared food and unsatisfactory snacks, and often we eat alone. This is where slow cooking comes into its own.

From your slow cooker the same specially prepared meal can be eaten by everyone in the family, whether separately or together, throughout the evening. The food, once cooked, stays hot and ready to serve. So you can go out to work in the morning knowing that an exciting and energy-saving dish awaits the family at supper-time.

Many of these recipes would be suitable for freezing, especially if the ingredients are doubled in quantity. So, as an added bonus, you can eat some straight away and save the rest for another day.

Honeyed Chicken

Use a chicken which is a snug fit. Herbs and spices impart flavour to the bird.

Serves 4–6   *LOW 8–10 hours*

2 large red onions
A large chicken, weighing about 2.25kg/5 lb
2 tbsp set honey
100g/3½ oz butter
2 tbsp wholegrain mustard
2 tbsp unsweetened orange juice
4 tbsp freshly chopped parsley
Freshly milled salt and pepper
6 rosemary sprigs
600ml/1 pint chicken stock

1. Preheat the slow cooker on High while you prepare the ingredients.

2. Finely chop the onions. If the chicken has been trussed, remove and discard the string and any excess fat from inside the body cavity. From the neck end push your fingers between the skin and flesh to make a cavity over the breast and the top of the legs.

3. In a small bowl mix together the honey, butter, mustard, orange juice, parsley and a little seasoning.

4. Place the chicken on a large plate or board and push the rosemary sprigs into the body cavity. Tilt the chicken with the neck end uppermost then spoon the honey mixture under the skin. With your fingers press and smooth the mixture evenly over the breast and legs. Don't worry if any flows out.

5. Scatter the chopped onion over the base of the slow cooker. Put the chicken on top, spooning over any excess honey mixture. Pour over the stock. Cover with the lid and cook on Low for 8–10 hours until the chicken is cooked through and almost falling off the bone.

6. With slotted spoons carefully lift the chicken onto a large plate, cover and keep warm. With a stick blender whizz the sauce until smooth.

7. Cut the chicken into portions and serve with the sauce poured over.

"Hunter's" Chicken

Based on the Italian dish Chicken Cacciatore, with chicken, tomatoes, onions, mushrooms, all cooked in white wine. Instead of wine, you could use cider or stock. Serve with crusty bread, couscous, polenta or mashed potatoes.

Serves 6   *LOW 4–6 hours*

2 tbsp plain flour
Salt and freshly milled black pepper
12 chicken thighs
2 medium onions
1 large red pepper
2 garlic cloves
150g/5½ oz mushrooms
1 tbsp olive oil
400g can chopped tomatoes
300ml/½ pint dry white wine
Few sprigs of fresh thyme

1.   Preheat the slow cooker on High while you prepare the ingredients.

2.   Season the flour with salt and pepper. Trim the chicken thighs of any excess skin and fat. Toss the chicken in the seasoned flour until well coated (we find this easiest to do in a large plastic food bag). Thinly slice the onions and red pepper, finely chop the garlic cloves and thickly slice the mushrooms.

3. Heat a large non-stick frying pan on the hob. When hot add the oil and half the chicken pieces, skin side down. Cook over high heat until the skin is golden brown and crisp. Lift out and set aside. Repeat with the remaining chicken.

4. Put the onions and pepper into the hot pan and cook over medium-high heat for about 5 minutes, stirring occasionally, until beginning to soften and turn golden brown. Add the garlic, mushrooms, tomatoes, wine and thyme. Bring just to the boil and transfer to the slow cooker.

5. Arrange the chicken pieces on top, skin side up, in an even layer and push them down gently into the vegetables.

6. Cover with the lid and cook on Low for 4–6 hours until the chicken and vegetables are very tender.

Curried Turkey & Sweet Potato Layer

This dish is equally good made with beef, pork or lamb mince in place of turkey.

Serves 4–6   *LOW 6–8 hours*

700g/1 lb 9 oz sweet potatoes
1 large red onion
2 garlic cloves
Small bunch of coriander
1 tbsp olive oil
1 tbsp cumin seeds
600g/1 lb 5 oz turkey mince
2 tbsp mild curry paste
2 tbsp tomato purée
300ml/½ pint passata
200g/7 oz garden peas
Freshly milled salt and black pepper
1 tbsp chicken bouillon powder
Extra chopped fresh coriander, to serve

1.   Preheat the slow cooker on High while you prepare the ingredients.

2.   Put the kettle on to boil. Peel and thinly slice the sweet potatoes. Finely chop the onion and garlic. Roughly chop the coriander.

3. Heat the oil in a wide non-stick pan and cook the cumin seeds for 1–2 seconds until they 'pop', immediately spoon onto kitchen paper. Add the onion and garlic to the pan and cook for 5 minutes until softened then add the minced turkey and cook for about 5 minutes until lightly brown, stirring and breaking up the meat with a wooden spoon. Stir in the coriander, cumin seeds, curry paste, tomato purée, passata, peas and a little seasoning. Mix thoroughly and remove from the heat. Put the bouillon powder in a jug and pour over 700ml/ 1¼ pints hot water.

4. Carefully scatter a third of the sliced potatoes in the base of the slow cooker pot. Cover with half of the turkey mix, repeat with the potato and meat mixture, ending with a layer of potato. Press down with the back of a spoon. Pour over the stock and cover with the lid.

5. Cook on Low for 6–8 hours. Sprinkle over extra coriander just before serving.

Beef & Pork Meat Loaf

This 'loaf' is cooked in a round cake tin. Tasty hot or cold.
Serve with salad, pickles and tiny hot potatoes.

Serves 6–8   *HIGH 4–6 hours*

Oil, for greasing
1 small red onion
1 garlic clove
1 red eating apple
Small bunch of parsley
4 sage leaves
350g/12 oz lean minced beef
150g/5½ oz lean minced pork
60g/2¼ oz fresh breadcrumbs
2 tbsp redcurrant jelly
2 medium eggs
Freshly milled salt and black pepper

1. Preheat the slow cooker on High while you prepare the
    ingredients.

2. Lightly grease and line the base of an 18cm/7 inch
    deep ovenproof dish with non-stick baking paper. Put
    the kettle on to boil. Finely chop the onion and garlic.
    Cut the apple into quarters, remove the cores and grate
    the fruit coarsely (there's no need to peel the apple).
    Finely chop the parsley and sage.

3. Heat a wide non-stick pan, and when hot tip in the minced beef and pork and cook for about 5 minutes until lightly brown, stirring and breaking up the meat with a wooden spoon. With a slotted spoon remove the mince and put on a plate. Add the onion and garlic to the pan and cook for 5 minutes until softened. Return the mince to the pan and stir in the apple and herbs.

4. Remove from the heat, cool for a few minutes and stir in the breadcrumbs, redcurrant jelly, eggs and seasoning. Spoon into the prepared dish.

5. Cover the dish tightly with foil and put into the slow cooker. Pour in sufficient hot water to come half-way up the sides of the dish. Cover with the lid and cook on High for 4–6 hours.

6. Lift the dish out of the slow cooker and leave to stand for 10 minutes. Loosen the edges with a knife and carefully turn out. Serve hot or cold, cut into slices.

Beef with Red Wine, Garlic & Thyme

Long slow cooking tenderises meat joints and allows flavours to develop. Melting and succulent, the meat starts to fall apart.

Serves 6–8   *LOW 8–10 hours*

A boned, rolled joint of brisket, weighing about 1.25kg/
    2¾ lb
3 medium onions
2 medium carrots
2 garlic cloves
150ml/¼ pint beef stock
450ml/16 fl oz red wine
1 tbsp wholegrain mustard
A few thyme sprigs
1 bay leaf
1 tsp freshly milled black pepper

1.   Preheat the slow cooker on High while you prepare the
      ingredients.

2.   Trim any excess fat from the joint of brisket. Finely chop
      the onions, thinly slice the carrots and crush the garlic.

3. Heat a large wide pan, and when hot add the brisket and brown quickly on all sides. Carefully lift into the slow cooker.

4. Tip the onions into the pan and cook for about 5 minutes until lightly browned, stirring occasionally.

5. Add the remaining ingredients to the browned onions and heat until bubbles begin to rise to the surface. Pour into the slow cooker over the meat.

6. Cover with the lid and cook on Low for 8–10 hours until the meat is tender and almost falling apart.

7. With slotted spoons carefully lift the brisket onto a large plate, cover and keep warm. Lift out and discard the woody thyme stalks and bay leaf. If you prefer a thicker sauce, use a stick blender and whizz until smooth.

8. Slice or tear the meat into pieces and serve with the sauce spooned over.

Leg of Lamb with Red Wine & Lentils

Choose a lamb joint that will fit your slow cooker – we usually ask our butcher to trim off the knuckle end of the leg. Serve with potatoes and a green salad or freshly cooked vegetables of your choice.

Serves 6   *LOW 6–9 hours*

200g/7 oz green lentils
1 medium onion
1 medium carrot
2 celery sticks
2 garlic cloves
A few fresh rosemary leaves
1 tbsp olive oil
1.5kg/3¼ lb leg of lamb
400g can chopped tomatoes
400ml/14 fl oz red wine
2 bay leaves
Salt and freshly ground black pepper

1. Put the lentils into a saucepan on the hob, cover well with water and boil rapidly for 10 minutes.

2. Preheat the slow cooker on High while you prepare the rest of the ingredients.

3. Drain the boiled lentils and put them into the slow cooker. Finely chop the onion, carrot, celery and garlic. Finely chop the rosemary – you will need about a teaspoonful.

4. Heat a large non-stick frying pan on the hob. When hot add the oil and brown the lamb quickly on all sides. Lift out onto a plate.

5. Add the onion, carrot, celery and garlic to the hot pan and cook over medium heat for 5–10 minutes until softened and just beginning to turn golden brown. Add the tomatoes, wine, rosemary, bay leaves and seasoning. Bring just to the boil and pour over the lentils in the slow cooker. Add the lamb and its juices and push it gently so that it nestles into the lentils.

6. Cover with the lid and cook on Low for 6–9 hours until the lamb and lentils are tender.

7. To serve, transfer the lamb to a warmed plate and carve. Taste the lentils and adjust the seasoning if necessary. Serve with the lamb.

Lamb Meatballs in Tomato Sauce

Serve with freshly cooked rice or spaghetti.

Serves 6   *LOW 4–6 hours*

Meatballs:
1 large onion
2 garlic cloves
Small handful of fresh mint leaves
Small handful of fresh parsley
1 large egg
800g/1¾ lb lean minced lamb
100g/3½ oz fresh breadcrumbs
1½ tsp ground cumin
Salt and freshly milled black pepper
Olive oil

Sauce:
1 small onion
1 small carrot
1 celery stick
1 tbsp olive oil
400g can chopped tomatoes
300ml/½ pint vegetable or chicken stock
1 tbsp tomato purée
1 tbsp sugar
Salt and freshly milled black pepper

1. To make the meatballs, finely chop the onion, garlic, mint and parsley. Lightly beat the egg. In a large mixing bowl, combine all the ingredients except the oil. Using wetted hands, shape the mixture into about 30 balls.

2. Preheat the slow cooker. Finely chop the onion, carrot and celery.

3. Heat a large non-stick frying pan on the hob. When hot, add a little oil and half the meatballs in a single layer. Cook quickly until golden brown all over. Transfer to the slow cooker and repeat with the remaining meatballs.

4. Add the oil to the hot frying pan with the onion, carrot and celery. Cook for about 5 minutes until golden brown. Stir in the remaining ingredients, bring just to the boil and pour the mixture over the meatballs in the slow cooker.

5. Cover with the lid and cook on Low for 4–6 hours.

Traditional Baked Beans with Pork

Haricot or navy beans are often used in recipes for traditional Boston baked beans. A piece of pork or bacon added to the beans is traditional and gives a depth of flavour. Serve with hot crusty bread.

Serves 6–8   *LOW 8–10 hours*

500g/1 lb 2 oz haricot beans
250g/9 oz pork or bacon
3 large onions
150ml/¼ pint passata
2 tbsp vegetable bouillon powder
2 tbsp dark brown sugar
2 tsp mustard powder
4 tbsp molasses (black treacle)
1 tsp freshly milled black pepper

1. Soak the beans overnight in plenty of cold water, or, alternatively, boil them in plenty of water for 2 minutes and leave to absorb the liquid for 2 hours.

2. Preheat the slow cooker on High while you prepare the ingredients.

3. Put the kettle on to boil. Trim excess fat from the pork or the rind from the bacon. Finely chop the onions. Drain the beans.

4. Heat a non-stick pan and when hot add the pork or bacon and brown quickly on all sides. Lift out with a slotted spoon.

5. Stir the remaining ingredients into the pan and pour over 700ml/1¼ pints boiling water. Bring back to the boil and cook for 10 minutes.

6. Transfer to the slow cooker and push the pork or bacon into the middle of the mixture. With the back of a spoon push the beans just under the liquid.

7. Cover with the lid and cook on Low for 8–10 hours until the meat is tender and the beans cooked through.

8. With a slotted spoon lift out the meat, cut into small pieces and return to the slow cooker. Stir and serve.

Sweet & Sour Pork

Serve with plenty of freshly cooked rice and perhaps a green salad. Any left over can be frozen for another time and reheated gently in a pan on the hob.

Serves 6–8   *LOW 5–8 hours*

1.4kg/3 lb lean pork
2 medium onions
2 garlic cloves
2 tbsp olive oil
250g can crushed pineapple
1 chicken stock cube
4 tbsp light soy sauce
2 tbsp red or white wine vinegar
2 tbsp sugar
Salt and freshly milled black pepper
3 tbsp cornflour
150ml/¼ pint dry sherry

1.   Preheat the slow cooker while you prepare the ingredients.

2.   Trim the pork and cut into large bite-size pieces. Slice the onions and finely chop the garlic.

3.   Heat a large non-stick frying pan on the hob. When hot, add 1 tbsp oil and the onions. Cook over medium heat for 5–10 minutes until beginning to soften and turn golden brown. Stir in the garlic and transfer to the slow cooker.

4.   Add the remaining 1 tbsp oil to the pan and brown the pork quickly in batches and transfer it to the slow cooker.

5.   To the hot frying pan add 500ml/18 fl oz water and the pineapple (including its juice), stock cube, soy sauce, vinegar, sugar and seasoning. While it heats, gradually blend the cornflour with the sherry to make a smooth paste and add to the pan. Stirring continuously, bring to the boil. Pour the thickened sauce over the contents of the slow cooker and stir well.

6.   Cover with the lid and cook on Low for 5–8 hours until very tender. Stir gently before serving.

Slow-Cooked Gammon

Use smoked or unsmoked gammon, as preferred, and you may like to soak the joint overnight in plenty of cold water first to help remove any excess salt. Serve it hot with boiled and buttered new potatoes and a tomato-and-onion salad. Or serve it cold as part of a buffet or Ploughman's Lunch, or sliced in sandwiches and salads. Once the gammon is cooked, you could glaze it by removing its rind, sprinkling the fat side with demerara sugar and browning quickly under a hot grill. The cooking juices could be made into a sauce by transferring them to a saucepan on the hob and blending in some cornflour, adjusting the seasoning to taste and adding a handful of finely chopped fresh parsley last minute.

Serves 6–8   LOW 4–6 hours

1 large onion
1 large carrot
2 celery sticks
1.8kg/4 lb gammon joint, soaked if wished (see note above) and drained
6 black peppercorns
4 whole cloves
2 bay leaves
A few parsley stalks
2 tbsp wholegrain mustard

1.   Preheat the slow cooker while you prepare the ingredients.

2.   Put the kettle on to boil. Thinly slice the onion, carrot and celery.

3.   Put the gammon into the slow cooker and scatter the onions and celery around the sides. Add the peppercorns, cloves, bay leaves and parsley stalks.

4.   Pour over about 400ml/14 fl oz boiling water (from the kettle) and stir in the mustard.

5.   Cover with the lid and cook on Low for 4–6 hours.

5

RELAX WITH FRIENDS

When entertaining friends you naturally want to rustle up something special by way of a feast. But how can you achieve this without being tied to the kitchen and ignoring your guests while you go quietly frantic?

Your secret weapon is your slow cooker. Slow cooking, for four, six, eight or more, lets you conjure up a dish with some wonderful, intense flavours and still gives you plenty of time to talk to your guests without a care in the world. Your friends might just wonder how you managed to feed them with so little apparent effort.

Even after a busy day your slow cooker makes it possible to invite friends round for dinner or supper. At weekends it is just the ticket for relaxed entertaining – good company and a delicious meal, enjoyed together at leisure.

Chicken & Prawns

This can easily be adjusted to serve six or eight, depending on the size of your slow cooker. Serve in shallow bowls with crusty bread for mopping up the juices.

Serves 4   *LOW 4–6 hours*

500g/1 lb 2 oz baby potatoes
2 celery sticks
2 medium leeks
1 medium carrot
1 garlic clove
4 anchovy fillets
400g can whole plum tomatoes
1 chicken stock cube
2 tbsp Worcestershire sauce
2 tsp sugar
4 chicken breasts
Salt and freshly milled black pepper
Small handful of sugar snap peas
½ lemon
Small handful of baby spinach leaves
About 200g/7 oz cooked shelled king prawns, with tails on
Extra virgin olive oil

1. Preheat the slow cooker on High while you prepare the ingredients.

2. Put the kettle on to boil. Thinly slice the potatoes, celery and the white parts of the leeks. Cut the carrot into small sticks. Finely chop the garlic and the anchovy fillets.

3. Put the prepared vegetables and anchovy fillets into the slow cooker and add the tomatoes, chopping them roughly as they go in. Dissolve the stock cube in 600ml/1 pint boiling water (from the kettle) and stir in the Worcestershire sauce and sugar. Pour the mixture over the contents of the slow cooker. Add the chicken breasts, pushing them down into the liquid. Season lightly.

4. Cover with the lid and cook on Low for 4–6 hours until the potatoes are tender.

5. Meanwhile, thinly slice the green leeks and thickly slice the sugar snap peas.

6. About 30 minutes before serving, adjust the seasoning to taste and squeeze in the juice from the lemon. Stir in the green leeks. Replace the lid and continue cooking for 20 minutes. Lift out the chicken and slice.

7. Stir in the chicken, sugar snap peas, spinach and prawns. Replace the lid and continue cooking for 10 minutes.

8. Drizzle a little olive oil over each serving.

Two-Cheese Fondue with Crispy Bacon

Here, everyone gathers around the slow cooker to dip crisp bread and vegetables into the creamy mixture of melted cheese and wine. If your slow cooker is a really large one, you may prefer to fondue ingredients in an ovenproof bowl, covered securely with foil. Stand it in the slow cooker and pour round sufficient boiling water (from the kettle) to come half-way up the sides of the dish and cook for the given time.

Serves 6   *LOW 1–3 hours*

300g/10½ oz Gruyère or Gouda cheese
300g/10½ oz Emmenthal cheese
1 large garlic clove
1 tbsp cornflour
300ml/½ pint dry white wine
Freshly grated nutmeg
Freshly milled white pepper
Few drops of chilli sauce
100g/3½ oz streaky bacon

To serve:
Crusty bread
Vegetables, such as sticks of carrot, pepper and cucumber; radishes, mange touts; wedges of Little Gem lettuce; chicory leaves

1. Preheat the slow cooker on High while you prepare the ingredients.

2. Grate the two cheeses. Cut the garlic clove in half and rub the cut sides over the inside of the slow cooker.

3. Put the grated cheeses into the slow cooker and stir in the cornflour. Add the white wine, a good pinch each of nutmeg and white pepper, and the chilli sauce. Stir well.

4. Cover with the lid and cook on Low for 1–3 hours.

5. Meanwhile, with scissors, trim the rind from the bacon rashers and cut into small strips. Put the bacon into a small non-stick frying pan and heat slowly until the fat begins to run. Increase the heat under the pan and cook quickly until the bacon is crisp and brown. Lift out onto kitchen paper to drain.

6. Just before serving, stir the crispy bacon pieces into the hot cheese mixture.

7. Serve with bread and vegetables for dipping.

Spiced Leg of Pork Cooked in Cider

Meat cooked on the bone has lots of flavour. Long slow cooking means the meat will almost fall off the bone and is amazingly tender. Serve with noodles or sautéed potatoes.

Serves 4–6   *LOW 6–8 hours*

1 leg of pork, to fit your slow cooker
2 medium leeks
3 tart apples
8 juniper berries
2 tsp ground cloves
2 tsp ground cinnamon
2 tsp ground ginger
150ml/¼ pint vegetable stock
300ml/½ pint sweet cider
Freshly milled salt and black pepper

1. Preheat the slow cooker on High while you prepare the ingredients.

2. Put the kettle on to boil. Trim excess fat from the pork and with a sharp knife make deep slits all over the meat. Thinly slice the leeks. Cut the apples into quarters, remove the cores and chop the fruit (there's no need to peel the apples). Crush the juniper berries.

3.   In a small bowl mix together the crushed juniper berries, ground cloves, cinnamon and ginger. Push this spice mix deep into the slits in the pork.

4.   Heat a wide non-stick pan and cook the pork until golden brown on all sides.

5.   Put the leeks and apples into the slow cooker and pour over the stock and cider and add a little seasoning. Put the pork on top and cover with the lid.

6.   Cook on Low for 6–8 hours. Lift the meat onto a hot plate, it will almost fall apart. Serve with the leeks and apples and some of the liquid.

Stuffed Shoulder of Lamb with Onion & Courgette Sauce

A succulent joint of meat with a caper, olive and walnut stuffing.

Serves 6–8   *LOW 6–8 hours*

1 boned shoulder of lamb
3 large red onions
2 large garlic cloves
4 courgettes

Stuffing:
2 tbsp capers
10 stoned black olives
10 walnut halves
Large bunch of parsley
1 large lemon

75cl bottle dry white wine
150ml/¼ pint lamb or chicken stock
Freshly milled salt and black pepper

1.   Preheat the slow cooker on High while you prepare the ingredients.

2.   Trim excess fat from the shoulder of lamb. Finely chop the onions and crush the garlic. Chop the courgettes. Chop the capers, olives, walnuts and parsley. Finely grate the rind from the lemon, cut in half and squeeze out the juice.

3. Put half of the lemon rind and juice into a bowl and mix in the remaining stuffing ingredients. Put the meat, skin side down, and spread the stuffing over. Fold the meat over and tie with string to secure.

4. Heat a wide non-stick pan, brown the lamb on all sides and remove. Add the onions, garlic and courgettes. Cook for 5 minutes until starting to brown. Stir in the remaining lemon rind and juice, wine, stock and seasoning. Heat until almost bubbling.

5. Pour into the slow cooker and place the joint on top. Cover with the lid and cook on Low for 6–8 hours.

6. Lift the lamb onto a hot plate. With a stick-blender whizz the vegetables and liquid until smooth. Spoon the sauce onto hot plates and top with slices of lamb.

Game Terrine

This flavourful savoury mix could be used to make meatballs or burgers.

Serves 4–6   *HIGH 4–6 hours*

**600g/1 lb 5 oz skinned, boneless mixed game meat,
    such as venison, rabbit, pigeon or pheasant**
2 rashers rindless smoked streaky bacon
1 small red onion
1 garlic clove
1 orange
Small bunch fresh parsley
2 sage leaves
1 tsp olive oil
50g/1¾ oz rolled oats
8 juniper berries
1 tbsp whisky or milk
100ml/3½ fl oz venison or chicken stock
1 medium egg
¼ tsp freshly milled black pepper

1. Preheat the slow cooker on High while you prepare the
    ingredients. Cut a large sheet of non-stick baking paper
    and a large sheet of extra thick foil.

2. Finely chop the meat, bacon, onion and garlic. Grate
    the rind from half the orange, squeeze juice from the
    whole orange. Chop the parsley and sage.

3. Heat the oil in a wide non-stick pan, and cook the meat and bacon for about 5 minutes until lightly brown. With a slotted spoon remove and put in a large bowl. Add the onion and garlic to the pan and cook for 5 minutes until softened. Remove from the heat and stir in the oats. Tip into the bowl of meat and mix in the remaining ingredients.

4. Put the sheet of baking paper on a clean surface and spoon the filling down the centre. Form into an oblong shape. Wrap the paper tightly around the mixture and then double wrap in foil, making sure it is well sealed.

5. Put into the slow cooker. Pour in sufficient hot water to almost cover the foil package. Cover with the lid and cook on High for 4–6 hours.

6. Lift the parcel out of the slow cooker and stand for 10 minutes. Unwrap and slice.

Spanish-Style Rice with Chicken, Mussels & Prawns

Based on the Spanish dish paella, in which saffron gives the rice its distinctive taste. This dish too is great for sharing with friends. A dressed green salad is the only accompaniment you may need.

Serves 6   LOW 2–3 hours

1 medium onion
2 garlic cloves
1 red pepper
6 boneless chicken thighs
About 150g/5½ oz spicy sausage, such as chorizo
2 tbsp olive oil
Pinch of saffron strands
1 chicken stock cube
1 generous tsp vegetable bouillon powder
500g/1 lb 2 oz easy-cook long grain rice
Freshly milled black pepper
About 12 cooked mussels in their shells
About 12 cooked, peeled king prawns, with tails on
Handful of frozen petits pois
2 ripe tomatoes
Chopped fresh parsley, to garnish

1.   Preheat the slow cooker on High.

2.   Put the kettle on to boil. Finely chop the onion and garlic. Halve the pepper, remove and discard its seeds and stalk, and cut into thin strips. Trim the chicken of any excess skin and fat. Thinly slice the sausage.

3. Heat a large non-stick frying pan on the hob. When hot add the oil and the chicken pieces, skin side down. Cook over medium to high heat until the skin is golden brown and crisp all over. Lift out and set aside.

4. Add the onion, pepper and garlic to the hot pan and cook over medium heat for about 5 minutes, stirring occasionally, until just beginning to soften. Stir in the saffron and sausage slices.

5. Dissolve the stock cube and bouillon powder in 1.2 litres/2 pints boiling water. Pour half the stock into the frying pan, bring just to the boil then transfer to the slow cooker. Stir in the remaining stock and rice. Season with black pepper. Add the browned chicken and its juices, gently pushing the pieces into the liquid.

6. Cover with the lid and cook on Low for 2–3 hours until the chicken is cooked through.

7. About 30 minutes before serving, stir in the mussels, prawns and petits pois.

8. Just before serving, finely chop the tomatoes and scatter them over the rice, together with some chopped parsley.

Bagna Cauda

We like to use the slow cooker to prepare things that often involve last-minute hassle – such as this rich anchovy and butter dish from Northern Italy. The mixture just sits there gently heating until we are ready to eat. Offer this dish as a starter or as a fun supper to share with friends – like a fondue, with bread and crudités.

Serves 6   LOW 1–3 hours

12 anchovy fillets in oil
4–6 garlic cloves
125g/4½ oz butter
250ml/9 fl oz extra virgin olive oil

To serve:
Plenty of crusty bread – offer a variety of types
Vegetables, such as sticks of carrot, pepper and
**   cucumber; radishes, mange touts; wedges of Little**
**   Gem lettuce; chicory leaves**

1.   Preheat the slow cooker on High while you prepare the ingredients.

2.   Put the kettle on to boil. Drain the anchovies and chop them into small pieces. Crush the garlic cloves. Cut the butter into small cubes.

3.   Put the anchovies and garlic into an ovenproof bowl and stir in the olive oil and butter. Cover the dish securely with foil and stand it in the slow cooker. Pour in sufficient water to come half-way up the sides of the bowl.

4.   Cover with the lid and cook on Low for 1–3 hours.

5.   Using a whisk, stir the mixture well until thick and well mixed.

6.   Serve with bread and vegetables for dipping.

Chilli Venison with Chocolate

No one would guess there's chocolate in this rich venison dish, with hot chillies and the sharp fruity flavours of cranberries. Chocolate is often added to traditional Mexican dishes. In place of the spices, chillies and chocolate use a spoonful of chilli chocolate sauce (see page 194).

Serves 6   *LOW 6–8 hours*

900g/2 lb stewing venison
3 rashers streaky bacon
12 shallots or pickling onions
2 red chillies (see page 15)
150g/5½ oz cranberries
¼ tsp ground nutmeg
¼ tsp ground allspice
1 bay leaf
1 cinnamon stick
400ml/14 fl oz venison or chicken stock
150ml/¼ pint port or red wine
¼ tsp freshly milled black pepper
55g/2 oz dark semi-sweet chocolate

1. Preheat the slow cooker on High while you prepare the ingredients.

2. Cut the venison into bite-sized pieces. With scissors snip the rinds from the bacon rashers and finely chop. Quarter the shallots or pickling onions. Cut the chillies in half, remove and discard their seeds and stalks, and slice thinly.

3. Put all the ingredients except the chocolate in the slow cooker.

4. Cover with the lid and cook on Low for 6–8 hours. Just before serving, remove the cinnamon stick and bay leaf, break the chocolate into pieces and stir into the dish until it has melted.

6

JUST YOU & ME?

Smart dishes for you and me, or maybe just for me!

A birthday, an anniversary, Valentine's Day, festivals and notable events – all are good excuses to push the boat out and take extra care to create a special slow-cooked meal for you and your partner. If you're dining solo, make a fuss of yourself to mark that special occasion. And, remember, your slow cooker is energy-saving compared to a meal for one or two taking hours in the oven.

Spend a little more money on fine ingredients, or go for size, like the whole salmon for the recipe on page 86, and splash the wine generously into the food when the recipe invites this. Then, topping up your glass and raising a toast, celebrate in style.

Seafood in a Wine & Herb Soup

A luxury main meal soup, ideal for two but can easily be halved to serve one. Ask the fishmonger for small pieces of different fish.

Serves 2　　　　　　　　　　　　　　*HIGH 1½–2½ hours*

1 medium red onion
2 garlic cloves
6 medium tomatoes
Small bunch fennel
Small bunch parsley
1 small lemon
300g/10½ oz mixed fish fillets, trout, bream or salmon
Pinch of saffron threads
1 tbsp fish or vegetable bouillon powder
300ml/½ pint red wine
2 tbsp tomato purée
Freshly milled salt and black pepper
200g/7 oz mixed shelled shellfish, prawns, cockles or
　　clams
1 tbsp capers
Hot crusty bread, to serve

1. Preheat the slow cooker on High while you prepare the ingredients.

2. Put the kettle on to boil. Finely chop the onion and crush the garlic. Roughly chop the tomatoes. Finely chop the herbs. Slice the lemon into 8 wedges. Cut the fish into bite-sized pieces.

3. Pour 150ml/¼ pint hot water into a jug and mix in the saffron threads, bouillon powder, wine, tomato purée and a little seasoning.

4. Put the onion, garlic and tomatoes evenly over the base of the slow cooker. Arrange the fish and shellfish on top. Scatter over the capers and half the chopped herbs. Pour over the wine mixture.

5. Cover with the lid and cook on High for 1½–2½ hours. Stir in the remaining chopped herbs just before serving in wide shallow bowls with hot crusty bread and lemon wedges.

Salmon & Prawns with Vermouth

A meal in a parcel. Salmon, prawns and vegetables with dill, lemon and vermouth flavourings cook in a paper and foil parcel with noodles cooking in the water alongside.

Serves 2   *HIGH 2–3 hours*

4 spring onions
6 button mushrooms
2 small carrots
100g/3½ oz mange tout
½ small lemon
3 tbsp dry vermouth
1 tbsp balsamic vinegar
Freshly milled salt and black pepper
2 handfuls spinach leaves
300g/10½ oz salmon fillet, in one piece
4 prawns, with shells
Sprigs of dill
150g/5½ oz noodles

1. Preheat the slow cooker on High while you prepare the ingredients. Cut a large sheet of non-stick baking paper three times the size of the fish fillet. You also need extra thick foil.

2. Put the kettle on to boil. Thinly slice the spring onions and mushrooms. Coarsely grate the carrots and cut the mange tout into long, thin strips. Cut the lemon into 4 slices.

3.   In a small bowl, mix the vermouth and balsamic vinegar with some seasoning.

4.   Put the sheet of baking paper on a clean surface and pile the spinach leaves in the centre and top with the other vegetables. Lay the fish fillet across the vegetables and put the prawns on top.

5.   Lift the paper up around the ingredients and scrunch to form a parcel, leaving space for the steam. Before you close the parcel, tuck the lemon slices and dill alongside the fish and pour over the vermouth mixture. Double wrap the parcel in foil.

6.   Put the parcel into the slow cooker. Pour in sufficient hot water to come half-way up the sides of the pot. Cover with the lid and cook on High for 2–3 hours. Stir in the noodles, cover and cook for a further 15 minutes.

7.   Lift the parcel from the cooker, carefully open to release the steam. With a slotted spoon remove and drain the noodles. Serve on hot plates.

Peppers with Spiced Cheese Stuffing

It may be necessary to trim the bases of the peppers to enable them to stand upright in the slow cooker – be careful you don't cut right through the flesh. Serve with a salad of crisp green leaves dressed with oil and vinegar.

Serves 2 as a main dish, 4 as a starter   *HIGH 2–4 hours*

100g/3½ oz bulgur wheat
1 generous tsp vegetable bouillon powder
4 red or yellow peppers or a mixture
1 small red onion
Small handful of fresh parsley
100g/3½ oz feta cheese
100g/3½ oz mozzarella or Cheddar cheese
2 tbsp toasted pine kernels
½ tsp mixed spice
2 tbsp sultanas
2 tsp Dijon mustard
1 tbsp extra virgin olive oil
Salt and freshly milled black pepper

1. Preheat the slow cooker on High while you prepare the ingredients.

2. Put the kettle on to boil. Put the bulgur wheat into a bowl. Dissolve the bouillon powder in 200ml/7 fl oz boiling water (from the kettle). Stir half the stock into the wheat and leave to stand for 10 minutes until the liquid has been absorbed. Reserve the remaining stock.

3. Cut the tops off the peppers and reserve. Remove and discard the seeds and white membranes. Put the peppers and their tops into a large heatproof bowl and pour over sufficient boiling water (from the kettle) to cover them. Leave to stand for 5 minutes before draining.

4. Finely chop the onion and parsley. Cut the cheeses into small cubes.

5. Mix the bulgur wheat, onion, parsley and cheeses with the pine kernels, mixed spice, sultanas, mustard, oil and seasoning. Pile the mixture into the peppers, stand them in the slow cooker and top them with their lids. Pour the reserved stock around.

6. Cover with the lid and cook on High for 2–4 hours.

Duck with Pomegranate Juice

Pomegranate juice is readily available in cartons or bottles. It adds a rich, tart, slightly sweet flavour to this dish.

Serves 2　　　　　　　　　　　　*LOW 2–4 hours + 15 minutes*

1 medium red onion
4 spring onions
2 large carrots
2 large courgettes
2 pak choi
2 duck breasts
2 tbsp cornflour
1 tbsp hoisin sauce
150ml/¼ pint pomegranate juice
150ml/¼ pint chicken stock
Freshly milled black pepper
150g/5½ oz noodles

1.　Preheat the slow cooker on High while you prepare the ingredients.

2.　Finely chop the onion. Cut the spring onions, carrots and courgettes into very thin strips. Finely shred the pak choi.

3. Heat a non-stick pan and cook the duck breasts until golden brown. Transfer the meat to a plate. Add the chopped red onion to the pan and cook for 5 minutes until beginning to brown. Stir in the cornflour, hoisin sauce, pomegranate juice, stock and a little seasoning. Heat until bubbling.

4. Arrange the vegetables over the base of the slow cooker. Put the duck breasts on top and pour over the onion and stock mixture.

5. Cover with the lid and cook on Low for 2–4 hours.

6. Whilst the dish is cooking, soak the noodles in water following the manufacturer's instructions. Drain the noodles, stir into the slow cooker, pushing them into the vegetables and liquid, cover and cook for a further 15 minutes.

Lamb Chops on Caramelised Squash

The slow cooker is ideal when you want small quantities of food to cook ever so slowly in their own juices. Simply put all your ingredients (browning them first when necessary) into an ovenproof dish, covered with foil and surrounded by hot water, and let it simmer away gently until you are ready to eat.

Serves 2   *LOW 4–6 hours*

1 small acorn squash
1 garlic clove
1 tbsp olive oil
15g/½ oz butter
1 tbsp soft light brown sugar
Pinch of chilli powder
4 lamb chops of your choice
Salt and freshly milled black pepper
10 cherry tomatoes
2 tbsp dry white wine
Lemon or lime wedges, to serve

1. Preheat the slow cooker on High while you prepare the ingredients.

2. Put the kettle on to boil. Chop the squash and crush the garlic. Heat a large non-stick frying pan on the hob. When hot, add the oil and butter, swirling it round until melted. Add the squash and garlic, sprinkle with the sugar and chilli powder and brown quickly on both sides until the sugar has caramelised slightly. Transfer to an ovenproof dish that will fit comfortably inside the slow cooker.

3. Add the lamb chops to the hot pan and brown quickly on all sides. Lift them out and lay them on top of the squash. Season with salt and pepper, scatter the tomatoes over and sprinkle the wine on top.

4. Cover the dish securely with foil and stand it in the slow cooker. Pour round sufficient boiling water to come half-way up the sides of the dish.

5. Cover with the lid and cook on Low for 4–6 hours.

6. Carefully lift the dish out of the slow cooker and remove the foil. Spoon the lamb, tomatoes and squash onto warmed plates and serve with lemon or lime wedges for squeezing over.

Lancashire Lamb Shanks

This is loosely based on the traditional recipe for Lancashire Hotpot, and includes more or less the same ingredients. You could jazz it up by adding a squeeze of lemon juice and a handful of black olives just before serving.

Serves 2   *LOW 8–10 hours*

1 medium onion
1 medium carrot
500g/1 lb 2 oz potatoes
1 tbsp olive oil
2 lamb shanks
15g/½ oz butter
Few sprigs of fresh thyme
Salt and black pepper
300ml/½ pint lamb stock or vegetable stock

1. Preheat the slow cooker on High while you prepare the ingredients.

2. Put the kettle on to boil. Chop the onion, thinly slice the carrot and cut the potatoes into small chunks.

3.   Heat a large non-stick frying pan. When hot, add the oil and the lamb shanks and brown quickly on all sides. Lift out onto a plate.

4.   Add the butter to the hot pan then toss in the onion, carrot and potatoes. Cook over medium heat for 8–10 minutes, stirring occasionally, until beginning to soften and brown.

5.   Add the thyme, seasoning and stock to the pan. Bring just to the boil and transfer to the slow cooker.

6.   Add the browned lamb shanks and their juices to the slow cooker, pushing them down snugly into the potatoes.

7.   Cover with the lid and cook on Low for 8–10 hours until very tender.

Pheasant in Orange & Apple Sauce

Choose a pheasant that will fit snugly into your slow cooker; alternatively, cut the bird into joints. Lovely with a salad of crisp chicory leaves, fresh orange segments and a few black olives.

Serves 2   *LOW 4–6 hours*

1 small onion
1 small orange
1 sharp eating apple
200g/7 oz chestnut mushrooms
1 tbsp olive oil
15g/½ oz butter
1 oven-ready pheasant, about 1.3kg/3 lb
25g/1 oz flour
300ml/½ pint chicken stock
150ml/¼ pint orange juice
150ml/¼ pint dry cider
Salt and freshly milled black pepper

1. Preheat the slow cooker on High while you prepare the ingredients.

2. Finely chop the onion. Finely chop the orange, skin and all, discarding any pips. Peel and quarter the apple, remove and discard its core, and cut into small pieces. Thickly slice the mushrooms.

3. Heat a large non-stick frying pan. When hot, add the oil and butter and brown the pheasant quickly all over. Transfer it to the slow cooker.

4. Add the onion, orange, apple and mushrooms to the hot pan and cook for 8–10 minutes, stirring occasionally, until beginning to soften and turn golden brown. Remove from the heat and stir in the flour. Gradually stir in the stock, orange juice and cider. Season with salt and pepper. Bring to the boil, stirring, and pour over the pheasant in the slow cooker.

5. Cover with the lid and cook on Low for 4–6 hours.

Mustard Chicken with Whisky & Wild Mushrooms

Smothered in a whisky and marmalade sauce, the flavours of Scotland permeate succulent chicken joints. Use free-range chicken for lots more taste.

Serves 2   *LOW 4–6 hours*

1 large red onion
200g/7 oz mixed wild mushrooms
6 thyme sprigs
2 tsp oil
2 chicken quarters
2 tbsp sesame seeds
2 tbsp wholegrain mustard
2 tbsp marmalade
2 tbsp whisky
300ml/½ pint chicken stock
Freshly milled salt and black pepper
2 tbsp double cream

1. Preheat the slow cooker on High while you prepare the ingredients.

2. Put the kettle on to boil. Finely chop the onion. If the mushrooms are large, tear into bite-sized pieces. Pull the leaves from the thyme sprigs.

3. Heat the oil in a pan and cook the chicken portions until golden brown on all sides. Transfer the chicken to the slow cooker. Add the onion to the pan and cook for 5 minutes until beginning to brown. Stir in the sesame seeds, mustard, marmalade, thyme leaves, whisky, stock and seasoning. Heat until almost bubbling.

4. Put the mushroom mixture into the slow cooker. Cover with the lid and cook on Low for 4–6 hours. Stir in the cream just before serving.

7

STRICTLY VEGETARIAN

Vegetables come in such a myriad of types and varieties, and, if you take in beans and lentils, tofu and Quorn, the range of flavours and textures is unending. Everyone, vegetarians and carnivores alike, will love these exciting, enticing and strictly vegetarian recipes.

These recipes are ideal for mid-week entertaining because they are so varied and adaptable. Complete in themselves, many could easily be served (to more people) as an accompaniment. And here's an idea for any non-veggies tempted to look in this section – some meat or fish would go really well with several of these recipes.

Stimulating and satisfying as they are, these are dishes for every season.

Flageolet & Black-Eyed Beans with Pistou

Pistou is the French version of Italy's pesto, a mix of olive oil, basil and garlic.

Serves 6–8   *LOW 6–8 hours*

250g/9 oz flageolet beans
250g/9 oz black-eyed beans
2 medium red onions
2 celery sticks
2 green chillies (see page 15)
1 lime
1½ tbsp vegetable bouillon powder
Freshly milled black pepper

Pistou topping:
6 tomatoes
2 garlic cloves
A small bunch fresh basil
60g/2¼ oz shelled walnut pieces
3 tbsp olive oil
Hot crusty bread, to serve

1. Soak the beans overnight in plenty of cold water.

2. Preheat the slow cooker on High while you prepare the ingredients. Put the kettle on to boil. Finely chop the onions and thinly slice the celery sticks. Cut the chillies in half, remove and discard their seeds and stalks, and slice thinly. Finely grate the rind from the lime. Cut the lime in half and squeeze out the juice.

3.   Drain the beans. Put into a large pan, cover with boiling water (from the kettle), bring back to the boil and cook rapidly for 10 minutes, then drain. Put the bouillon powder into a measuring jug and pour over 700ml/1¼ pints boiling water.

4.   Put the beans into the slow cooker and add the prepared vegetables, chillies and lime rind and juice, then stir in the stock and season with pepper. Cover with the lid and cook on Low for 6–8 hours.

5.   Whilst the dish cooks, prepare the topping. Put the tomatoes into a bowl, cover with boiling water (from the kettle) and leave for 1–2 minutes until the skins start to shrivel. With a slotted spoon lift out the tomatoes and leave to cool a little. With a sharp knife pull off the skins, cut in half, remove the cores and finely chop. Tip into a small dish, cover and chill until needed.

6.   Finely chop the garlic, basil leaves and walnuts. Put them into a small dish, pour over the oil, season a little then cover and chill until needed.

7.   Serve the bean mixture in wide bowls topped with a spoonful of tomato, a little pistou and lots of crusty bread.

Root Vegetables & Red Beans in Spiced Coconut Sauce

The vegetables can be varied to suit your taste. Serve with freshly cooked rice or in shallow bowls with chunks of crusty bread. Any left over can be reheated the next day in the microwave or in a pan on the hob.

Serves 6   *LOW 6–8 hours*

2 medium onions
2 garlic cloves
2.5cm/1 inch piece of ginger root
2 medium leeks
2 medium carrots
2 medium parsnips
500g/1 lb 2 oz celeriac
200ml block of creamed coconut
410g can red kidney beans
2 tbsp olive oil
1 tsp cumin seeds
500ml/18 fl oz vegetable stock
1 generous tbsp curry paste
1 tsp ground turmeric
Salt and freshly milled black pepper
Handful of fresh coriander leaves

1. Preheat the slow cooker on High while you prepare the ingredients.

2. Thinly slice the onions and finely chop the garlic cloves. Finely grate the root ginger. Cut the leeks, carrots, parsnips and celeriac into bite-size pieces. Cut the coconut into small pieces. Drain the beans.

3. Heat a large saucepan on the hob. When hot add the oil, onions, garlic, ginger and cumin seeds. Cook over medium heat for about 8 minutes or until beginning to soften and turn golden brown.

4. Add the leeks, carrots, parsnips and celeriac to the pan. Stir in the coconut, stock, curry paste, turmeric, seasoning and red beans. Bring just to the boil, stirring occasionally, and transfer to the slow cooker.

5. Cover with the lid and cook on Low for 6–8 hours.

6. Just before serving, roughly chop the coriander leaves and stir them in.

Spiced Beetroots & Red Cabbage with Tofu

Beetroots are often overlooked as a hot vegetable, possibly because they colour the other ingredients. Here we've teamed them with other red or orange vegetables, given them a spicy taste and added tofu for extra protein.

Serves 4–6   *LOW 3–5 hours + 15–20 minutes*

2 medium red onions
1 garlic clove
½ medium red cabbage
6 medium beetroots
1 small orange
300g/10½ oz firm tofu
300ml/½ pint vegetable stock
3 tbsp red wine vinegar
3 tbsp clear honey
2 tsp chilli sauce
2 tsp dried mixed herbs
¼ tsp ground cloves
Freshly milled salt and black pepper
Crème fraîche, to serve
Chopped fresh parsley, to serve

1. Preheat the slow cooker on High while you prepare the ingredients.

2. Finely chop the onions and crush the garlic. Cut the red cabbage in half, remove and discard the central core then thinly shred. Trim any stalks from the beetroots then remove the skin with a potato peeler. (Wear disposable gloves when handling beetroots to prevent your hands becoming discoloured.) Coarsely grate the beetroots. Finely grate the rind from the orange, cut in half and squeeze out the juice. Dice the tofu and chill until needed.

3. Pour the stock into a jug and stir in the vinegar, honey, chilli sauce, orange rind and juice, mixed herbs, cloves and a little seasoning.

4. Tip the vegetables into the slow cooker and pour over the stock mixture. Cover with the lid and cook on Low for 3–5 hours. Stir after the first 2 hours.

5. Stir in the tofu and cook for a further 15–20 minutes. Serve with a dollop of crème fraîche and sprinkle over a little parsley.

Vegetable Chilli with Pan-Fried Tofu

We sometimes like to fry tofu for a brown, crisp result, as in this recipe. You could, of course, leave the tofu as it is and stir it into the chilli for the final half to one hour of cooking. A suitable accompaniment might be rice, couscous or thick slices of crusty bread (plain or spread with garlic butter and toasted).

Serves 6   *LOW 5–7 hours*

1 large onion
1 medium carrot
1 large celery stick
1 garlic clove
1 red pepper
1 yellow pepper
1–2 small red chillies (see page 15)
Two 425g cans red kidney beans
3 tbsp olive oil
Two 400g cans chopped tomatoes
450ml/¾ pint vegetable stock
2 tbsp tomato purée
Salt and freshly milled black pepper
Two 250g packets marinated or smoked firm tofu

1. Preheat the slow cooker on High while you prepare the
    ingredients.

2. Finely chop the onion, carrot, celery and garlic. Halve
    the peppers, remove the seeds and stalks, and slice
    thickly. Finely chop the chillies. Drain the kidney beans.

3. Heat 1 tbsp oil in a large pan on the hob and add the onion, carrot, celery and garlic. Cook over medium heat for 8–10 minutes, stirring occasionally until beginning to soften and turn golden brown.

4. Stir in all the ingredients except the remaining oil and the tofu. Bring just to the boil and tip into the slow cooker.

5. Cover with the lid and cook on Low for 5–7 hours until the vegetables are very soft.

6. About 30 minutes before serving, drain the tofu and pat it dry with kitchen paper. Cut into bite-size cubes or strips. Heat the remaining 2 tbsp oil in a non-stick frying pan, add the tofu in batches, browning it quickly on all sides. Lift out and keep warm.

7. Serve the vegetable chilli topped with the browned tofu.

Quorn Cassoulet

Hot garlic bread goes very well with this hearty meat-free dish.

Serves 6   *LOW 4–6 hours + 1 hour*

2 medium onions
1 medium carrot
2 celery sticks
2 garlic cloves
Three 425g cans haricot beans
2 tbsp olive oil
450ml/16 fl oz vegetable stock
2 tbsp tomato purée
2 tbsp wholegrain mustard
2 tbsp black treacle
Salt and freshly milled black pepper
Two 300g packets Quorn pieces, thawed if frozen
6 Quorn sausages, thawed if frozen

Topping:
25g/1 oz butter
6 tbsp fresh breadcrumbs
Small handful of chopped fresh parsley

1. Preheat the slow cooker on High while you prepare the ingredients. Thinly slice the onions, carrot and celery. Finely chop the garlic. Drain the beans.

2. Heat a large saucepan. When hot add the oil, onions, carrot and celery. Cook over medium heat for 8–10 minutes until beginning to soften and turn golden brown. Stir in the garlic and beans. Add the stock, tomato purée, mustard, treacle and seasoning. Bring just to the boil and transfer to the slow cooker.

3. Cover with the lid and cook on Low for 4–6 hours until the vegetables are very tender.

4. Meanwhile, heat the butter in a small non-stick pan and cook the breadcrumbs until crisp and golden. Stir in the parsley and leave to cool.

5. Stir in the Quorn pieces and sausages, replace the lid and continue cooking for 1 hour. Serve sprinkled with the topping.

Minestrone Stew

Though this is meant to be a main dish, it could also be served as a starter, with some crusty Italian-style bread such as ciabatta. To jazz it up, consider grilling cheese on thick slices of toast and serving them on top of the stew or, for meat eaters, you could stir in some crisp-fried bacon pieces or meaty sausages.

Serves 6–8   *LOW 8–10 hours*

2 large onions
2 garlic cloves
2 large carrots
3 celery sticks
2 leeks
1 fennel bulb
410g can cannellini or haricot beans
410g can chickpeas
3 tbsp olive oil
500g carton passata
1 litre/1¾ pints vegetable stock
Salt and freshly milled black pepper
¼ Savoy cabbage
Handful of fresh parsley
Hard Parmesan-style cheese
Handful of small pasta shapes, such as shells

1. Preheat the slow cooker on High while you prepare the ingredients.

2. Finely chop the onions and garlic. Thickly slice the carrots, celery, leeks and fennel. Drain the beans and chickpeas.

3. Heat the oil in a large saucepan on the hob. Add the onions, garlic, carrots and celery and cook for about 10 minutes, stirring occasionally, until just beginning to soften and turn golden brown.

4. Add the leeks, fennel, beans, chickpeas, passata, stock and seasoning. Bring just to the boil and tip into the slow cooker.

5. Cover with the lid and cook on Low for 8–10 hours until the vegetables are tender.

6. Meanwhile, slice the cabbage very thinly and chop the parsley. With a potato peeler, shave off strips of the cheese.

7. About 30 minutes before serving, stir in the cabbage and pasta. Replace the lid and cook for a further 30 minutes until the pasta is soft.

8. Stir in the parsley and serve in bowls topped with cheese shavings.

Marrow with Bulgur Wheat, Pepper & Ginger Stuffing

A retro dish with an up-to-date filling.

Serves 4   *LOW 2–4 hours*

1 marrow

Stuffing:
60g/2¼ oz bulgur wheat
1 medium onion
1 garlic clove
1 medium red pepper
Small piece fresh root ginger
2 tbsp small raisins
2 tbsp pine nuts
1 tbsp light soy sauce
2 tbsp chopped fresh herbs
Freshly milled salt and black pepper

400g can chopped tomatoes
400ml/14 fl oz chicken or vegetable stock
Chopped fresh parsley to serve

1. Preheat the slow cooker on High.

2. Put the kettle on to boil. Cut the marrow into thick slices, about 8cm/3¼ inches and scoop out the seeds. (Check they fit into the slow cooker in a single layer.) Tip the bulgur wheat into a bowl and pour in boiling water to cover. Chop the onion and crush the garlic. Cut the pepper in half, remove and discard the seeds and stalks, and finely chop. Grate the ginger root.

3. Drain the bulgur wheat in a sieve, pressing down with the back of a spoon to remove as much water as possible. Tip into a large bowl and stir in the rest of the stuffing ingredients, seasoning a little.

4. Spoon and press the stuffing into the marrow rings. Pour the tomatoes and stock into the slow cooker and stir to mix. With a fish slice carefully lift the marrow rings into the slow cooker (a little stuffing may escape but don't worry).

5. Cover with the lid and cook on Low for 2–4 hours. Carefully lift the marrow slices onto plates. Spoon over the sauce and sprinkle with parsley.

Creamy Squash & Sweet Potato Casserole

This could just as easily be made entirely with sweet potatoes or with squash. It may not be the most attractive dish in the world but it tastes wonderful and we like the way the vegetables mash into the juices to give a chunky-yet-smooth texture. Serve it in shallow bowls with crusty bread for mopping up the creamy juices.

Serves 4–6   *LOW 2½–3½ hours + 30 minutes*

1 red onion
800g/1¾ lb sweet potatoes
800g/1¾ lb squash, such as acorn or butternut
2 garlic cloves
2.5cm/1 inch piece of fresh ginger root
About 4 sun-dried tomatoes
1 tbsp vegetable bouillon powder
Freshly milled black pepper
2 medium courgettes
Small handful of mange touts
150ml/¼ pint double cream
Handful of fresh coriander leaves

1. Preheat the slow cooker on High while you prepare the ingredients.

2. Put the kettle on to boil. Finely chop the onion. Peel and cut the sweet potatoes into chunks. Peel and discard the seeds from the squash and cut the flesh into chunks. Finely chop or crush the garlic cloves. Finely grate the ginger root. Cut the sun-dried tomatoes into small strips.

3. Put the onion, sweet potatoes, squash, garlic, ginger root, bouillon powder, black pepper and tomatoes into the slow cooker and stir in 600ml/1 pint boiling water (from the kettle).

4. Cover with the lid and cook on Low for 2½–3½ hours until the vegetables are soft.

5. Meanwhile, thinly slice the courgettes and cut the mange touts into short lengths.

6. Gently stir the courgettes, mange touts and cream into the cooked vegetables, replace the lid and continue cooking for a further 30 minutes.

7. Just before serving, stir in the coriander leaves.

Lentils, Root Vegetables, Star Anise & Lemon

A robust, rustic dish which couldn't be simpler to prepare. Adapt the dish by using seasonal vegetables. Serve as a veggie meal with hot crusty garlic bread, with a sprinkling of grated cheese, or to accompany a curry dish or roast meats.

Serves 6–8   *LOW 6–8 hours*

250g/9 oz lentils
2 large onions
2 large garlic cloves
3 medium parsnips
2 small turnips
1 large unwaxed lemon
1 tbsp dried mixed herbs
700ml/1¼ pints vegetable stock
10 peppercorns
2 star anise
1 bay leaf

1. Preheat the slow cooker on High while you prepare the ingredients.

2. Wash the lentils in plenty of cold water and drain. Finely chop the onions and crush the garlic. Peel, trim and chop the parsnips and turnips into even-sized smallish pieces. Cut the lemon into 6 wedges.

3. Put all the ingredients into the slow cooker. Cover with the lid and cook on Low for 6–8 hours. Stir twice after the first 2 hours. The lentils will soften and thicken the dish. Remove the bay leaf and star anise before serving.

Aubergines, Potatoes & Carrots with Lemon Myrtle

Lemon myrtle is an Australian spice and adds a distinctive lemon flavour to dishes. Replace with lemon rind if you can't find it in the stores.

Serves 4–6, or 6–8 as an accompaniment   *LOW 4–6 hours*

1 red onion
500g/1 lb 2 oz carrots
2 aubergines, weighing about 450g/1 lb
1 kg/2¼ lb small new potatoes
Small bunch of fresh parsley
500g carton passata
1½ tbsp vegetable bouillon powder
3 tsp ground lemon myrtle
Freshly milled salt and black pepper

1. Preheat the slow cooker on High while you prepare the ingredients.

2. Put the kettle on to boil. Finely chop the onion and carrots. Trim the stalks from the aubergines and chop into even sized-pieces. Leaving the skins on, cut each potato into quarters. Finely chop the parsley.

3. Tip the vegetables into the slow cooker and scatter over half of the parsley (save the remainder for later).

4. Add the passata, bouillon powder and lemon myrtle and pour over 700ml/1¼ pints boiling water.

5. Stir well, cover with the lid and cook on Low for 4–6 hours.

6. Stir in the remaining parsley and season if necessary.

8

PERFECT PASTA, RICE & GRAINS

Here are some dishes to prove how versatile your slow cooker can be – probably more so than you imagined. Most of these pasta, noodle and rice dishes cannot be left alone for hours and hours like the typical slow cooker dish; they are quicker to prepare, but will need your attention.

These recipes are great for the middle of the week, when time is at a premium, so put the slow cooker on straight away when you come home from work.

We've used an exciting selection of ingredients, including millet and barley which you might not have tried before.

Pasta, Mushroom & Bean Medley

This dish relies on ingredients tucked away in the store-cupboard and makes an ideal midweek supper that is quick to put together. Keep it veggie or make some last-minute additions: flaked canned tuna, torn pieces of roast chicken, chopped ham, or freshly cooked sausages hot from the grill or frying pan. Garlic bread goes well with it.

Serves 4–6   *LOW 5–8 hours + 30 minutes*

1 red onion
1 red or yellow pepper
285g jar mixed mushrooms in oil
265g can flageolet beans
400g can tomatoes
2 tbsp soy sauce
1 tbsp vegetable bouillon powder
2 tsp sugar
250g/9 oz pasta twists

1. Preheat the slow cooker on High while you prepare the ingredients.

2. Put the kettle on to boil. Finely chop the onion. Cut the pepper in half, remove and discard the seeds and stalk, and slice thinly. Drain the mushrooms and beans.

3. Put the onion, pepper, mushrooms and beans into the slow cooker and add the tomatoes, soy sauce, vegetable bouillon powder and sugar. Stir in 750ml/1¼ pints boiling water (from the kettle).

4. Cover with the lid and cook on Low for 5–8 hours.

5. Switch the slow cooker to High. Stir in the pasta twists, pushing them under the surface of the liquid. Replace the lid and continue cooking on High for about 30 minutes, stirring gently once or twice, or until the pasta is just soft.

Trout & Fennel Pasta

There's such a huge choice of pasta shapes; for a change, try coloured pasta, flavoured with beetroot, spinach, squid or herbs. Serve with salad leaves.

Serves 4 -6   *HIGH 2–3 hours*

4 spring onions
1 green pepper
1 large fennel bulb
3 celery sticks
½ lemon
300g/10½ oz trout fillets
1 tbsp fish or vegetable bouillon powder
350g/12 oz green spinach-flavoured pasta or plain pasta
  spirals
Freshly milled salt and pepper

1. Preheat the slow cooker on High while you prepare the ingredients.

2. Slice the spring onions. Halve the green pepper, remove the seeds and slice thinly. Finely chop the fennel and celery sticks. Grate the rind from the lemon and squeeze out the juice. Cut the trout into bite-size pieces.

3. Put the kettle on to boil. Put the bouillon powder into a jug and pour over 700ml/1¼ pints hot water.

4. Put the onions, pepper, fennel, celery, lemon rind and juice into the slow cooker. Pour over the stock.

5. Cover with the lid and cook on High for 2–3 hours. Then, 35–45 minutes before serving stir the pasta and trout into the slow cooker pushing it under the liquid, re-cover and cook until tender. Season if necessary before serving.

Oriental Chicken with Egg Noodles

A lovely light dish that couldn't be easier to make. The star anise and cinnamon stick subtly add their flavours to the sauce, which is allowed to soak into the egg noodles shortly before serving.

Serves 4–6   LOW 3–5 hours + 10 minutes

8–12 skinned chicken thighs
2.5cm/1 inch piece of fresh ginger root
5 tbsp dry sherry
3 tbsp brown sugar
5 tbsp soy sauce
1 star anise
1 cinnamon stick
300ml/½ pint chicken stock
250g packet of medium egg noodles
A few spring onions, to serve

1.   Preheat the slow cooker on High while you prepare the ingredients.

2.   Trim the chicken thighs of any excess fat. Finely grate the ginger root.

3.   Put 300ml/½ pint water into a saucepan on the hob and add the sherry, sugar, soy sauce, star anise, ginger root, cinnamon stick and stock. Bring just to the boil and transfer to the slow cooker.

4. Add the chicken thighs to the slow cooker, pushing them into the liquid.

5. Cover with the lid and cook on Low for 3–5 hours until the chicken is very tender.

6. Move the chicken to the sides of the slow cooker and add the noodles, pushing them gently under the surface of the liquid. Replace the lid and continue cooking for about 10 minutes, stirring and separating the noodles once or twice, until soft and ready to serve.

7. Finely chop some spring onions and scatter over the chicken and noodles to serve.

Mushroom & Parmesan Rice

Dried mushrooms are a useful store-cupboard stand-by and we like the added flavour they give to dishes. Use small pieces in this risotto and choose from oyster, portobello, morel and chanterelle, to name just a few. Or use 250g/9 oz fresh mushrooms.

Serves 4–6   *LOW 1–2 hours*

350g/12 oz easy-cook long grain rice
1 red onion
1 garlic clove
8 asparagus spears
70g/2½ oz Parmesan cheese
50g/1¾ oz butter
2 tsp olive oil
½ tsp dried thyme
70g/2½ oz dried mushrooms
Freshly milled salt and pepper
1½ tbsp vegetable bouillon powder

1. Preheat the slow cooker on High while you prepare the ingredients.

2. Put the kettle on to boil. Rinse the rice under running cold water and drain. Thinly slice the onion and crush the garlic. Cut the asparagus into short lengths. Grate the Parmesan cheese.

3. Heat the butter and oil in a medium pan and fry the onion for a few minutes until softened. Add the garlic and rice and cook, stirring, for 2 minutes. Stir in the thyme, mushrooms, asparagus and seasoning. Add the bouillon powder and pour over 1.2 litres/2 pints hot water.

4. Pour into the slow cooker. Cover with the lid and cook on Low for 1–2 hours, stirring gently after 1 hour. Before serving stir in the Parmesan cheese.

Chilli Brown Rice with Prawns & Seeds

Brown rice is very nutritious and nutty. Sunflower and sesame seeds add crunch to this chilli prawn dish.

Serves 4   *LOW 3–4 hours*

1 medium red onion
350g/12 oz easy-cook long grain brown rice
300ml/½ pint vegetable stock
300ml/½ pint tomato juice
1 tbsp chilli paste
1 tbsp Worcestershire sauce
Freshly milled salt and pepper
200g/7 oz spinach leaves
250g/9 oz shelled prawns
Small handful sunflower seeds
Small handful pumpkin seeds

1. Preheat the slow cooker on High while you prepare the ingredients.

2. Finely chop the onion.

3. Put the onion and rice into the slow cooker and pour over the stock and tomato juice. Stir in the chilli paste, Worcestershire sauce and seasoning.

4. Cover with the lid and cook on Low for 3–4 hours. Then, 15–20 minutes before the end of the cooking time stir in the spinach leaves, prawns, sunflower and pumpkin seeds.

Brown Rice with Leeks, Bacon & Cheese

We like to use brown rice though you could, of course, use white instead (but make sure you use the easy-cook variety for best results). Serve it like risotto – as a starter or with a salad garnish as a main dish.

Serves 4–6   *HIGH 1–1½ hours*

250g/9 oz easy-cook brown rice
2 medium leeks
1 garlic clove
200g/7 oz button or chestnut mushrooms
About 200g/7 oz back bacon rashers
2 tbsp olive oil
700ml/1¼ pints vegetable or chicken stock, or a mixture
About 125g/4½ oz mature Cheddar-style cheese
Chopped fresh parsley

1. Preheat the slow cooker on High while you prepare the ingredients.

2. Wash and drain the rice. Thinly slice the leeks and finely chop the garlic clove. Halve or thickly slice the mushrooms. With scissors, trim the rind from the bacon rashers and cut into small strips.

3. Heat a large non-stick frying pan on the hob. When hot add the oil and bacon. Cook over medium-high heat for about 5 minutes until just beginning to brown.

4. Add the leeks and garlic to the bacon and cook over medium heat for about 5 minutes, stirring occasionally, until the leeks have softened slightly but not browned.

5. Stir in the rice, then add the mushrooms and stock. Bring just to the boil and tip the mixture into the slow cooker, stirring gently.

6. Cover with the lid and cook on High for 1–1½ hours, stirring gently after 1 hour, until the rice is just soft and almost all the liquid has been absorbed.

7. Meanwhile, grate the cheese.

8. Serve topped with grated cheese and chopped parsley.

Lamb Couscous

Couscous is made from the grain of semolina and used in North African cuisine. Serve with hot breads and mango chutney.

Serves 4–6   *LOW 2½–3½ hours*

1 large red onion
2 garlic cloves
2 carrots
1 celery stick
1 courgette
100g/3½ oz okra
4 dried apricots
500g/1 lb 2 oz boneless lean lamb
2 tsp olive oil
½ tsp ground cumin
½ tsp ground ginger
2 tsp lamb bouillon powder
Freshly milled salt and pepper
350g/12 oz couscous
85g/3 oz pine nuts
1 tbsp fresh parsley

1. Preheat the slow cooker on High while you prepare the ingredients.

2. Finely chop the onion and garlic. Thinly slice the carrots, celery and courgette. Trim the okra. Quarter the apricots. Trim excess fat from the lamb and cut into bite-size pieces.

3. Put the kettle on to boil. Heat the oil in a large frying pan, add the lamb and cook for a few minutes until golden brown. Remove the lamb to a plate. Fry the onion and garlic until brown, stir in the carrots, celery, courgette, okra and apricots. Mix in the cumin, ginger, bouillon powder and seasoning and pour over 600ml/1 pint hot water. Heat until starting to bubble. Put into the slow cooker.

4. Cover with the lid and cook on Low for 2½–3½ hours. Meanwhile, tip the couscous into a large bowl and pour over cold water to cover. Then, 5–10 minutes before the end of the cooking time, drain the couscous and stir with the pine nuts and parsley into the slow cooker and replace the lid. Stir again before serving.

Barley Pilaff with Lamb & Mushrooms

Barley and lamb combine to make a dish that is richly flavoured and filling. Serve it with a crisp green salad.

Serves 4–6   *LOW 4–6 hours + HIGH 1–1½ hours*

1 large onion
1 medium carrot
1 garlic clove
150g/5½ oz chestnut mushrooms
Small sprig of fresh rosemary
4–6 lamb leg steaks, each weighing about 175g/6 oz
1 tbsp olive oil
150ml/¼ pint dry white wine or vermouth
500ml/18 fl oz lamb or vegetable stock
Salt and freshly milled black pepper
250g/9 oz pearl barley

1.   Preheat the slow cooker on High while you prepare the ingredients.

2.   Finely chop the onion, carrot and garlic. Slice the mushrooms. Finely chop the rosemary leaves to make about 1 tsp. Cut each lamb steak into about 4 pieces.

3.   Heat a large non-stick frying pan on the hob. When hot add the oil and the lamb in a single layer. Brown quickly on all sides and lift onto a plate.

4.   Add the onion, carrot, garlic and mushrooms to the hot pan and cook over medium heat for about 5 minutes or until beginning to soften and turn golden brown.

5.   Stir in the rosemary and wine or vermouth and bubble quickly for a few seconds. Add the stock and a little seasoning. Bring just to the boil and transfer to the slow cooker. Add the lamb and its juices, pushing it down into the liquid.

6.   Cover with the lid and cook on Low for 4–6 hours until the lamb and vegetables are tender.

7.   Switch the slow cooker to High and stir in the barley. Replace the lid and cook on High for a further 1–1½ hours or until the barley is tender.

Hot Cracked Wheat & Ham Salad

In place of ham, try adding thickly sliced smoked sausage.
Any left-over salad can be served cold.

Serves 4–6   *HIGH 1 hour + 15 minutes*

250g/9 oz bulgur wheat
1 medium onion
1 medium leek
1 tbsp olive oil
25g/1 oz butter
700ml/1¼ pints vegetable or chicken stock, or a mixture
2 tbsp Worcestershire sauce
2 tbsp tomato purée
1 tsp dried mint or a generous tbsp finely chopped fresh
  mint
4 small courgettes
4 tomatoes
Small handful of pine kernels
4–6 thick slices of cooked ham
Salt and freshly milled pepper

1. Put the bulgur wheat into the slow cooker and preheat it
    on High while you prepare the other ingredients.

2. Thinly slice the onion and leek.

3. Heat the oil and butter in a saucepan. Add the onion
    and leek and cook over medium heat for 5–10 minutes
    until softened and just beginning to turn golden brown.

4.   Stir the stock into the onion mixture, together with the Worcestershire sauce, tomato purée and mint. Bring just to the boil and pour over the wheat in the slow cooker, stirring gently.

5.   Cover with the lid and cook on High for 1 hour or until nearly all the liquid has been absorbed.

6.   Meanwhile, finely chop the courgettes and tomatoes. Lightly toast the pine kernels in a dry frying pan until golden brown. Chop the ham.

7.   Stir the courgettes, tomatoes and ham into the hot wheat, replace the lid and continue to cook for a further 15 minutes.

8.   Season if necessary and serve topped with toasted pine kernels.

Warm Millet Salad

Millet is a cereal grass and often overlooked as an ingredient. Be careful not to overcook it. Delicious with other salad ingredients, or use as a filling for tortillas, pancakes or pitta bread.

Serves 4–6   *HIGH 1–2 hours*

6 spring onions
1 garlic clove
250g/9 oz millet seeds
2 tsp olive oil
1 tbsp mild curry paste
1 tbsp lime juice
1 tbsp vegetable bouillon powder
Small handful broken walnut pieces
Freshly milled salt and pepper
Large bag mixed small salad and herb leaves

1. Preheat the slow cooker on High while you prepare the ingredients.

2. Thinly slice the spring onions and garlic.

3. Heat a non-stick pan and when hot add the millet and 'toast' for a few seconds until golden and put to one side. (Watch it doesn't burn.)

4. Pour the oil into the pan, fry the spring onions and garlic for a few minutes until softened. Stir in the curry paste, lime juice, bouillon powder, walnuts and seasoning. Tip the millet back into the pan and pour over 700ml/1¼ pints hot water. Heat until boiling.

5. Pour into the slow cooker. Cover with the lid and cook on High for 1–2 hours. Stir in the salad leaves and serve immediately. (The leaves will wilt.)

9

HOT & SPICY, EASY PEASY!

The spices of the world can find their way into your slow cooker, and you can have a 'take-away' from your own kitchen on any day you choose and at any time you like. It's cheaper too, and the food can be guaranteed to be top quality, with ingredients sourced from your favourite supermarket, corner shop or specialist store.

Whether your fancy runs to Indian, Mexican, Chinese or Thai cuisine, you'll find something to entice and excite you on this global menu. Just add the appropriate sidelines to your 'take-away' – bread (nan or tortillas), poppadoms, pickles, chutneys and relishes – and the world is at your fingertips.

Tarka Dhal

A well-flavoured dish of creamy split peas and squash. For the 'tarka', onions and garlic are cooked in oil and tipped onto the dhal just before serving. It goes well with rice, nan bread or poppadums, chutneys, tomato and red onion salad, plain yogurt flavoured with freshly chopped mint, or with roast vegetables.

Serves 6–8   *LOW 8–10 hours*

250g/9 oz yellow split peas
500g/1 lb 2 oz piece of squash, such as butternut or
   acorn
1 large onion
2 garlic cloves
2 red chillies (see page 15)
2 tomatoes
1cm/½ inch piece fresh ginger root
2 tbsp oil
1 tsp ground coriander
1 tsp ground cumin
1 tsp tamarind paste
Salt and freshly milled black pepper
1 tbsp fresh lemon juice

For the 'tarka':
1 small onion
2 garlic cloves
3 tbsp oil

1. Soak the peas in plenty of cold water for several hours or overnight.

2. Preheat the slow cooker on High while you prepare the ingredients.

3. Drain the split peas. Remove and discard the peel and seeds from the squash and cut it into thin slices. Finely chop the onion, garlic and chillies. Chop the tomatoes and finely grate the root ginger.

4. Heat the oil in a large saucepan, add the onion, garlic and chillies and cook over medium heat for about 8 minutes, stirring occasionally, until slightly softened.

5. Add the coriander and cumin and cook, stirring, for 1 minute. Add the split peas, squash, tomatoes, ginger, tamarind paste, seasoning and 1 litre/1¾ pints water. Boil for 5–10 minutes and transfer to the slow cooker.

6. Cover with the lid and cook on Low for 8–10 hours until the peas are very soft. When stirred, the mixture should break up into a porridge-like consistency (for an extra smooth dhal, whizz the mixture with a hand-held stick blender). Adjust the seasoning to taste and stir in the lemon juice.

7. Meanwhile, thinly slice the onion for the tarka and finely chop the garlic. Just before serving, heat the oil in a frying pan and cook the onion and garlic over medium heat until soft and golden brown. Tip the tarka on top of the dhal to serve (take care because the mixture can spit ferociously as it hits the peas).

Biryani

A spicy fragrant feast-day meal cooked in one dish. Bags of frozen mixed shellfish work well here and, in place of individual spices, use a curry powder or paste. Serve with yogurt, pickles and nan bread to scoop up the rice mixture.

Serves 6   *LOW 4–6 hours*

1 large red onion
2 garlic cloves
Small piece fresh root ginger
250g/9 oz basmati rice
2 tbsp oil
½ tsp ground chilli powder
½ tsp ground cumin
½ tsp ground coriander
3 cardamom pods
1 tbsp lemon juice
1 tbsp vegetable bouillon powder
350g/12 oz mixed shelled shellfish
3 tbsp sultanas
3 tbsp freshly chopped parsley
Freshly milled black pepper
Toasted flaked almonds, to serve

1. Preheat the slow cooker on High while you prepare the ingredients.

2. Put the kettle on to boil. Finely slice the onion and garlic. Grate the ginger root. Wash the rice under running cold water and drain.

3. Heat the oil in a large frying pan, add the onion and garlic, cook for a few minutes until golden brown. Add the spices and rice and cook for 2 minutes, stirring continuously. Mix in the lemon juice, bouillon powder, pour over 400ml/14 fl oz water and bring just to the boil. Spoon into the slow cooker.

4. Cover with the lid and cook on Low for 4–6 hours. Then, 30 minutes before serving, stir in the shellfish, sultanas and parsley and re-cover. Season if necessary and serve topped with flaked almonds.

Chickpeas with Cumin, Green Chillies & Parsley

The chickpeas are best soaked overnight before cooking, so start preparing the evening before. Though the rosemary is optional, it makes a lovely addition to the finished flavour. Serve with couscous or rice.

Serves 6   *LOW 8–10 hours*

350g/12 oz dried chickpeas
1 large onion
2 garlic cloves
2 green chillies (see page 15)
2.5cm/1 inch piece fresh ginger root
2 tbsp olive oil
1 tbsp cumin seeds
1 tsp turmeric
1 sprig of fresh rosemary (optional)
150ml/¼ pint dry white wine or vermouth
400g can chopped tomatoes
700ml/1¼ pints vegetable stock
Salt and freshly milled black pepper
Handful of fresh flat-leaf parsley

1. Soak the chickpeas in plenty of cold water for at least 8 hours or overnight. Next day, drain them and put them into a large saucepan on the hob. Cover well with water and boil rapidly for 10 minutes.

2. Preheat the slow cooker on High while you prepare the rest of the ingredients.

3. Finely chop the onion, garlic and chillies. Finely grate the ginger root.

4. Heat the oil in a large pan on the hob and add the onion, garlic and cumin seeds. Cook over medium heat for 5–10 minutes, stirring occasionally, until lightly browned.

5. Stir in the chillies, ginger, turmeric and rosemary (if using) and cook for 1 minute. Add the wine or vermouth, bubble quickly for a few seconds, and then stir in the tomatoes, stock and a little seasoning. Drain the boiled chickpeas and stir them in. Bring the mixture just to the boil and transfer to the slow cooker.

6. Cover with the lid and cook on Low for 8–10 hours.

7. Before serving, adjust the seasoning to taste, roughly chop the parsley and stir it in.

Thai Green Chicken & Vegetable Curry

Serve spooned over fragrant rice.

Serves 4–6   *LOW 4–6 hours*

1 large onion
1 carrot
2 celery sticks
1 red pepper
200g/7 oz green beans
1 garlic clove
2.5cm/1 inch piece fresh ginger root
1 lime
4–6 skinless, boneless chicken breasts
2 tbsp oil
1 tbsp Thai green curry paste
300ml/½ pint chicken or vegetable stock
2 tbsp light soy sauce
200ml/7 fl oz coconut milk
Handful of fresh coriander leaves

1.   Preheat the slow cooker on High while you prepare the ingredients.

2.   Thinly slice the onion, carrot and celery. Halve the pepper, remove and discard the seeds and stalk, and chop roughly. Trim the beans and cut them into short lengths. Finely chop the garlic and finely grate the ginger root. Finely grate the rind from the lime and squeeze out its juice. Cut each chicken breast into about six pieces.

3.   Heat the oil in a large non-stick pan and add the onion, carrot and celery. Cook over medium heat for 5–10 minutes, stirring occasionally, until softened and just beginning to brown.

4.   Stir in the curry paste, garlic and ginger and cook for 1 minute.

5.   Add the remaining ingredients, except for the coconut milk and coriander. Bring just to the boil and transfer to the slow cooker, pushing the ingredients down into the liquid.

6.   Cover with the lid and cook on Low for 4–6 hours until the chicken and vegetables are tender. About 30 minutes before serving, stir in the coconut milk. Just before serving, stir in the coriander leaves.

Chilli Chicken Bowl

This resembles the Chinese dish Chow Mein with a dash of chilli added. We have used dried chillies but you could, of course, use fresh (see page 15). Adjust the amount to suit your palate. The noodles are already cooked and just need stirring in before serving.

Serves 4–6   *LOW 4–6 hours + 10–15 minutes*

1 onion
2 carrots
2 garlic cloves
2.5cm/1 inch piece fresh ginger root
340g can sweetcorn
225g can bamboo shoots
4–6 boneless, skinless chicken breasts
1 tbsp oil
5 tbsp soy sauce, plus extra for serving
1 tbsp sugar
Generous pinch of crushed chillies
300g packet of fresh bean sprouts
300g packet of straight-to-wok noodles
2 tsp sesame oil (optional)
Toasted sesame seeds, to serve

1. Preheat the slow cooker on High while you prepare the ingredients.

2. Finely chop the onion. Cut the carrots into short sticks. Finely chop the garlic. Finely grate the ginger root. Drain the sweetcorn and bamboo shoots. Cut each chicken breast into five or six pieces.

3. Heat the oil in a large frying pan on the hob. Add the onion, carrots, garlic and ginger root and cook over medium-high heat for 3–5 minutes, until just beginning to turn golden brown. Add the drained sweetcorn and bamboo shoots, the soy sauce, sugar and chillies, and 400ml/14 fl oz water. Bring just to the boil, stir in the chicken and transfer to the slow cooker.

4. Cover with the lid and cook on Low for 4–6 hours.

5. Gently stir in the bean sprouts, noodles and sesame oil (if using), replace the lid and continue cooking for 10–15 minutes.

6. Serve topped with toasted sesame seeds and hand round the soy sauce for sprinkling over.

Chicken Dhal

Dhal is usually served as an accompaniment to a curry. Here it takes centre stage. Serve with rice, pickles and hot nan bread.

Serves 4–6   *LOW 3–5 hours*

1 medium red onion
1 garlic clove
1 red chilli (see page 15)
4 skinned, boned chicken breasts
1 tbsp oil
200g/7 oz red lentils
300ml/½ pint chicken stock
300ml/½ pint coconut milk
1 tsp ground ginger
1 tsp ground cumin
1 tsp ground coriander
6 cardamom pods

1. Preheat the slow cooker on High while you prepare the ingredients.

2. Finely chop the onion and garlic. Cut the chilli in half, remove and discard the seeds and stalks, and slice thinly. Cut the chicken into strips.

3. Heat the oil in a frying pan, add the onion and cook over medium heat for a few minutes until just beginning to soften. Stir in the garlic. Increase the heat, add the chicken and cook, stirring occasionally, until golden brown.

4. Put the chicken mixture into the slow cooker and stir in the remaining ingredients.

5. Cover with the lid and cook on Low for 3–5 hours.

Chilli Beef & Chorizo

Quick and easy to prepare. Serve with hot crusty garlic bread, jacket potatoes or spaghetti, and extra chilli sauce for those who prefer it hotter.

Serves 4   *HIGH 3–5 hours*

1 large onion
2 garlic cloves
150g/5½ oz spicy sausage, such as chorizo or kabanas
250ml/9 oz lean minced beef
400g can chickpeas
200g/7 oz sweetcorn
400g can chopped tomatoes
1 tsp chilli sauce
2 tsp beef bouillon powder
Freshly milled salt and black pepper
Natural yogurt, to serve

1.   Preheat the slow cooker on High while you prepare the ingredients.

2.   Finely chop the onion and crush the garlic. Thinly slice the sausage.

3.   Heat a non-stick pan, and, when hot, tip in the sausage and beef and cook for about 5 minutes until lightly brown, stirring and breaking up the meat with a wooden spoon. With a slotted spoon remove the meat and put onto a plate. Add the onion and garlic to the pan and cook for 5 minutes until softened. Return the meat to the pan and stir in the chickpeas, sweetcorn, tomatoes, chilli sauce, and bouillon powder. Pour over 300ml/½ pint hot water and heat until starting to bubble. Tip into the slow cooker.

4.   Cover with the lid and cook on High for 3–5 hours. Season if necessary and serve with a little yogurt spooned on top.

Spiced Lamb with Apricots

Succulent lamb flavoured with curry powder and cumin. Serve with couscous or rice.

Serves 6   *LOW 6–8 hours*

2 medium onions
2 garlic cloves
1 red pepper
150g/5½ oz dried apricots
2 tbsp plain flour
2 tbsp curry powder
1 tsp ground cumin
1 tsp ground turmeric
½ tsp salt
1kg/2¼ lb lean lamb cubes
2 tbsp oil
400g can chopped tomatoes
1 generous tsp vegetable bouillon powder
2 tbsp lemon juice

1. Preheat the slow cooker on High while you prepare the ingredients.

2. Finely chop the onions and garlic. Halve the pepper, remove and discard the seeds and stalk, and chop roughly. Halve the dried apricots.

3. Mix together the flour, curry powder, cumin, turmeric and salt and toss the lamb cubes in the mixture (easy to do in a large plastic food bag).

4. Heat the oil in a large non-stick frying pan. Quickly brown the lamb in batches and transfer to the slow cooker.

5. Add the onions and garlic to the hot pan and cook over medium heat for about 8 minutes, stirring occasionally, until just beginning to soften and brown. Add the red pepper, apricots, tomatoes, bouillon powder and 300ml/½ pint water. Bring just to the boil and stir the mixture into the lamb in the slow cooker, pushing the apricots under the surface.

6. Cover with the lid and cook on Low for 6–8 hours until the lamb and vegetables are very tender. Stir in the lemon juice just before serving.

Chinese Pork with Cashews

Serve with rice and pickled ginger root.

Serves 4–6   *LOW 3–5 hours*

6 spring onions
Small piece of root ginger
1 red pepper
1 red chilli (see page 15)
200g/7 oz mange tout
350g/12 oz lean boneless pork
1 tbsp cornflour
1 tbsp olive oil
150ml/¼ pint chicken stock
1 tbsp clear honey
1 tbsp tamarind paste
Large handful bean sprouts
12 cashew nuts

1. Preheat the slow cooker on High while you prepare the ingredients.

2. Thinly slice the spring onions. Peel or scrape the ginger root and finely grate. Cut the pepper and chilli in half, remove and discard their seeds and stalks, and slice thinly. Cut the mange tout diagonally into strips. Cut the pork into thin slices and dust with the cornflour.

3. Heat the oil in a frying pan, add the spring onions and cook over medium heat for a few minutes, stirring occasionally, until just beginning to soften. Stir in the ginger, red pepper and chilli. Increase the heat, add the pork and cook, stirring occasionally, until golden brown.

4. Put the pork mixture into the slow cooker, stir in the stock, honey and tamarind paste. Heat until just bubbling. Pour into the slow cooker.

5. Cover with the lid and cook on Low for 3–5 hours. Then, 30 minutes before serving stir in the mange tout and bean sprouts, cashew nuts and re-cover.

Mild Lamb Curry with Coconut

Equally good made with chicken in place of lamb. Serve with rice, mango chutney and pickles.

Serves 4   *LOW 3–5 hours*

500g/1 lb 2 oz boneless, lean lamb
1 tbsp olive oil
400g chopped tomatoes
¼ tsp turmeric
¼ tsp cayenne pepper
½ tsp ground cloves
½ tsp ground cinnamon
300ml/½ pint coconut milk
150ml/¼ pint vegetable stock
150ml/¼ pint crème fraîche

1.   Preheat the slow cooker on High while you prepare the ingredients.

2.   Cut the lamb into bite-size pieces.

3.   Heat the oil in a frying pan, add the lamb and cook until golden brown. Stir in the remaining ingredients except the crème fraîche and heat until starting to bubble.

4.   Pour into the slow cooker. Cover with the lid and cook on Low for 3–5 hours. 10 minutes before serving stir in the crème fraîche.

10

LEISURELY PUDS

There's a special appeal about puddings – they are so comforting and mouthwatering that they make you want to settle down and relax in order to savour them to the full. We love old-fashioned puddings, though we've given some of our recipes an up-to-date twist; there's plenty of fruit, and lots of sweetness and stickiness. If you have a sweet tooth then just get stuck in; if you're health-conscious you can still find something here with just a hint of indulgence.

On weekdays or on special occasions these puddings are equally delicious, and they go well throughout the year too, summer and winter alike.

Some of these dishes are cooked straight in the slow cooker. For others the mixture is put into a dish which is then placed inside the slow cooker, surrounded by hot water. This technique is used for Sticky Butterscotch Pudding (page 166) and Egg Custard with Lime & Maple Syrup (page 171).

Pecan-Filled Apples

Check that the apples will fit inside your slow cooker. For a change replace the apples with firm pear halves.

Serves 4   *HIGH 2–4 hours*

4 small Bramley cooking apples
90g/3¼ oz pecan nuts
2 tbsp clear honey
1 tsp ground ginger
25g/1 oz butter
150ml/¼ pint unsweetened apple juice

1. Preheat the slow cooker on High while you prepare the ingredients.

2. With a sharp knife score around the fattest part of the apples and remove the cores. Finely chop the pecan nuts.

3. In a bowl, mix together the nuts, honey and ginger. Spoon the mix into the apples, pressing it down well and top each with a little butter.

4. Arrange the apples in the slow cooker and pour over the apple juice.

5. Cover with the lid and cook on High for 2–4 hours.

Plums & Berry Crumble

Fruit crumble is an age-old pudding which never seems to be out of fashion. The rubbed-in crumble topping mix freezes really well without setting into a solid mass. Spoon onto prepared fruits and cook.

Serves 4–6   *HIGH 2–4 hours*

600g/1 lb 5 oz red plums
140g/5 oz plain wholemeal flour
40g/1¾ oz rolled oats
½ tsp ground cinnamon
90g/3¼ oz butter
90g/3¼ oz soft brown sugar
300g/10½ oz raspberries and blackberries or
  blueberries

1. Preheat the slow cooker on High while you prepare the ingredients.

2. Halve and stone the plums.

3. Mix the flour, oats and cinnamon in a large bowl. Cut the butter into small cubes and add to the flour mixture. Using your fingertips, rub in the butter until the mixture resembles fine crumbs (or do this part in a food processor). Stir in 40g/1½ oz of the sugar.

4. Arrange the plums, raspberries and blackberries over the base of the slow cooker pot. Sprinkle over the remaining sugar and 6 tbsp cold water. Cover with the crumble mixture, but don't press it down too firmly.

5. Cover with the lid and cook on High for 2–4 hours.

Brioche, Banana & Cranberry Pudding

Odd but true: jam, sultana and custard sandwiches on top of banana and cranberries. Warming, comforting and very very tempting. We used fresh cranberries, but frozen are available all year round. Ring the changes with other seasonal fruits.

Serves 4–6   HIGH 2–3 hours

40g/1½ oz butter, plus extra for greasing
1 orange
4 large bananas
140g/5 oz cranberries
3 tbsp soft brown sugar
8 thick slices sweetened bread (brioche)
2 tbsp apricot jam
500g carton custard
Handful sultanas
2 medium eggs
400ml/14 fl oz milk
Extra custard, to serve

1.   Preheat the slow cooker on High while you prepare the ingredients.

2.   Lightly grease the inside of the slow cooker pot. Finely grate the rind from the orange, cut the orange in half and squeeze out the juice. Thinly slice the bananas.

3. Put the cranberries and banana slices into the slow cooker, sprinkle over the sugar and pour over the orange juice. Lightly butter a slice of bread, spread with some apricot jam and a little custard and scatter over a few sultanas. Cover with a slice of bread to make a 'sandwich' and cut in half. Repeat with the remaining bread slices.

4. Arrange the sandwiches evenly over the top of the fruit. Beat the eggs into the milk and pour over the pudding.

5. Put the dish into the slow cooker. Pour in sufficient hot water to come half-way up the sides of the dish. Cover with the lid and cook on High for 2–3 hours. Serve with extra custard.

Chocolate Ginger Pudding

Serve this sticky pudding with a generous spoonful of thick yogurt, crème fraîche or custard; or our favourite – a scoop of vanilla ice cream.

Serves 4–6   *HIGH 3–4½ hours*

100g/3½ oz soft butter, plus extra for greasing
2 medium eggs
4 large pieces of stem ginger in syrup
100g/3½ oz soft brown sugar
150g/3½ oz self-raising flour
25g/1 oz cocoa powder

1. Preheat the slow cooker on High while you make the pudding.

2. Put the kettle on to boil. Butter the inside of a 1.2 litre/2 pint pudding bowl. Lightly beat the eggs. Drain the ginger and chop into small pieces.

3. Beat the butter with the sugar until light and fluffy. Gradually beat in the eggs. Sift the flour and cocoa powder over the top and, with a large metal spoon, fold in gently, adding the chopped ginger and 1–2 tbsp of the syrup from the jar.

4.	Spoon the mixture into the prepared bowl. Cover with a sheet of non-stick baking paper and then a sheet of foil. Scrunch up the edges, pressing them onto the sides of the bowl to make a secure seal.

5.	Stand the bowl in the slow cooker and pour in sufficient boiling water (from the kettle) to come half-way up the sides of the bowl

6.	Cover with the lid and cook on High for 3–4½ hours until gently firm to the touch and cooked through.

7.	Carefully lift the bowl from the slow cooker. Turn the pudding out onto a warmed plate for serving.

Tropical Fruit Pudding

This pudding is served straight from the slow cooker. Putting a sheet of non-stick paper under the lid helps prevent condensation from dripping onto the sponge as it cooks. Accompany it with pouring cream, yogurt, ice cream or hot custard.

Serves 6–8   *HIGH 2½–3½ hours*

125g/4½ oz soft butter, plus extra for greasing
1 small pineapple
1 ripe mango
2 large bananas
2 passion fruit
125g/4½ oz soft light brown sugar
2 medium eggs
Few drops of vanilla extract
150g/5½ oz self-raising flour
25g/1 oz desiccated coconut

1. Rub the inside of the slow cooker with a little butter then preheat on High while you prepare the ingredients.

2. Prepare the pineapple by cutting off the top and base, and removing and discarding the skin, including the 'eyes'. Cut the trimmed fruit into quarters lengthways and remove and discard the hard core. Cut the remaining fruit into small chunks. Peel the mango, slice the flesh from the stone and chop roughly. Peel and thickly slice the bananas.

3. Put the pineapple, mango and banana in an even layer in the slow cooker. Halve the passion fruit and, using a teaspoon, scrape the seeds and juice over the top.

4. Put the butter, sugar, eggs and vanilla extract into a large mixing bowl and sift the flour over the top. Beat well for 2–3 minutes until light and smooth, and then fold in the coconut.

5. Spoon the mixture evenly over the fruit in the slow cooker (no need to level the surface).

6. Place a large sheet of non-stick paper over the top and secure it down with the lid.

7. Cook on High for 2½–3½ hours until the sponge is firm to the touch.

Squash & Raisin Pudding

The squash gives its sweetness to this pudding and helps to keep it moist. Carrot would work just as well. Serve warm with thick cream, yogurt or custard, or a quick fruit sauce made by blending a can of apricots in light syrup.

Serves 6–8   *HIGH 2½–3½ hours*

3 tbsp pine kernels
150g/5½ oz soft butter, plus extra for greasing
150g/5½ oz squash, such as butternut, weighed after
   peeling and discarding seeds
3 medium eggs
150g/5½ oz soft light brown sugar
150g/5½ oz self-raising flour
½ tsp baking powder
1 tsp ground mixed spice
3 tbsp sultanas or raisins
3 tbsp milk

1.   Preheat the slow cooker on High while you prepare the ingredients.

2.   Put the kettle on to boil. In a small non-stick frying pan, lightly toast the pine kernels until golden brown and leave to cool. Butter the inside of a 17.5–20cm/7–8 inch ovenproof soufflé dish or deep cake tin and line its base with a circle of non-stick baking paper. Grate the squash. Lightly beat the eggs.

3. Beat the butter with the sugar until light and fluffy. Gradually beat in the eggs. Sift the flour, baking powder and mixed spice over the top and, with a large metal spoon, fold in. Lightly fold in the grated squash, sultanas or raisins, toasted pine kernels and milk.

4. Spoon the mixture into the prepared dish. Cover with a sheet of non-stick baking paper and then a sheet of foil. Scrunch up the edges, pressing them onto the sides of the dish to make a secure seal.

5. Stand the dish in the slow cooker and pour in sufficient boiling water (from the kettle) to come half-way up its sides.

6. Cover with the lid and cook on High for 2½–3½ hours until firm to the touch and cooked through.

Chocolate & Rum Fondue

This is sheer indulgence and chocoholics' idea of heaven! Give your guests long-handled forks for spearing marshmallows and the like for dipping into the molten chocolate. We like to use a chocolate with at least 50 per cent cocoa solids. Sometimes, we replace the rum with brandy or orange liqueur. This mixture also makes a luxurious sauce to serve with fruit or ice cream.

Serves 4–6   *LOW 1 hour + 30 minutes*

200g/7 oz dark chocolate
150ml/¼ pint double cream
3 tbsp golden syrup
3 tbsp rum

To serve – choose a selection:
Marshmallows
Cubes of crusty bread
Cubes of cake, such as Madeira or sweet brioche
Sponge fingers
Crisp biscuits or cookies
Nuts, such as Brazils, walnuts or pecan halves
**Fresh fruit, such as orange segments, chunks of fresh
   pineapple, banana**
Dried fruit, such as apricots or dates

1. Preheat the slow cooker on High while you prepare the ingredients.

2. Put the kettle on to boil. Break the chocolate into a heatproof bowl and add the cream and golden syrup. Cover securely with foil.

3. Put the bowl into the slow cooker and pour round sufficient boiling water (from the kettle) to come half-way up its sides.

4. Cover with the lid and cook on Low for 1 hour.

5. Stir well and replace the foil securely. Replace the lid and continue cooking for a further 30 minutes.

6. Just before serving, stir in the rum.

7. Serve with your chosen selection of 'dippers'.

Sticky Butterscotch Pudding

Custard is our favourite accompaniment for this rather sophisticated pudding. Best results come if the dates are soaked and cooled before adding them to the pudding mixture.

Serves 6–8   *HIGH 3½–4½ hours*

Topping:
25g/1 oz butter, plus extra for greasing
50g/1¾ oz soft brown sugar
5 tbsp double cream

Pudding:
175g/6 oz pitted dates
1 tea bag, such as Earl Grey
2 medium eggs
85g/3 oz soft butter
115g/4 oz soft brown sugar
Few drops of vanilla extract
150g/5 oz self-raising flour

1. Chop the dates and put them into a small bowl with the tea bag. Pour over 120ml/4 fl oz boiling water (from the kettle). Cover and leave to cool.

2. Preheat the slow cooker on High while you prepare the rest of the ingredients.

3. Put the kettle on to boil. Butter a deep 15–18cm/6–7 inch ovenproof dish (such as a soufflé dish) and line the base with a circle of non-stick paper. Lightly beat the eggs.

4. To make the topping, melt the butter and stir in the sugar and cream. Spread the mixture over the paper in the dish.

5. To make the pudding, beat the butter with the sugar until light and fluffy. Gradually beat in the eggs and vanilla extract. Sift the flour over the top and, with a large metal spoon, fold in lightly.

6. Remove the tea bag from the dates, squeezing it to release any liquid. Stir the dates and their juices into the pudding mixture. Spoon it into the dish (no need to level the surface).

7. Cover with a sheet of non-stick paper and then a sheet of foil. Scrunch the edges tightly to the sides of the dish, securing them well.

8. Stand the dish in the slow cooker and pour round sufficient boiling water (from the kettle) to come half-way up its sides.

9. Cover with the lid and cook on High for 3½–4½ hours until firm to the touch and cooked through.

10. Run a knife round the side of the dish and turn the pudding out onto a warmed plate. Remove the paper and serve.

Plum Pudding

This pudding, with its dumpling topping, is suitable for all sorts of fruit – try rhubarb, apples, raspberries or cherries. The amount of sugar depends on the sweetness of the fruit. To make a smaller pudding, halve the quantities and assemble it in a suitable sized ovenproof dish. Cover securely with non-stick paper and foil, and put into the slow cooker with boiling water to come half-way up its sides.

Serves 8   *LOW 3–5 hours + HIGH 45 minutes*

1kg/2¼ lb plums
8 tbsp elderflower cordial
4 tbsp caster sugar, plus extra if necessary

Topping:
200g/7 oz self-raising flour
1 tsp baking powder
50g/1¾ oz butter
2 tbsp caster sugar
1 medium egg
100ml/3½ fl oz milk
2 tbsp demerara sugar

1. Preheat the slow cooker while you prepare the fruit.

2. Halve the plums and remove and discard their stones. Put the fruit into the slow cooker and stir in the cordial and 2 tbsp water. Sprinkle with the sugar.

3. Cover with the lid and cook on Low for 3–5 hours until very soft.

4. To make the topping, sift the flour with the baking powder. Using fingertips, rub in the butter until the mixture resembles fine breadcrumbs. Stir in the sugar. Lightly beat the egg with the milk and stir into the flour mixture to make a soft dough.

5. Taste the plum mixture and adjust the sweetness if necessary.

6. Drop eight spoonfuls of the dough on top of the hot fruit (do not spread them out).

7. Cover with the lid and cook on High for 45 minutes until the topping is firm to the touch and cooked through.

8. Leave to stand, uncovered, for 5 minutes before sprinkling with the demerara sugar and serving.

Chocolate Rice Pudding

Delicious hot, by itself or with poached fruits, or cold, topped with yogurt or cream.

Serves 4–6   *HIGH 4–6 hours*

Butter, for greasing
140g/5 oz pudding rice
3 tbsp cocoa powder
150ml/¼ pint coconut milk
1 litre/1¾ pints milk
90g/3¼ oz raisins
60g/2¼ oz sugar
½ tsp vanilla extract
60g/2¼ oz semi-sweet chocolate
Toasted flaked almonds, to serve

1. Put the kettle on to boil. Grease the inside of the slow cooker. Rinse the rice in cold water.

2. Put the cocoa into a small bowl and stir in 3 tbsp hot water. Mix until smooth and stir in 3 tbsp cold water.

3. Put all of the pudding ingredients, except the chocolate and the almonds, into the slow cooker.

4. Cover with the lid and cook on High for 4–6 hours, stirring once or twice during the final 2 hours. Stir in the chocolate until melted and serve scattered with almonds.

Egg Custard with Lime & Maple Syrup

All the flavour of crème caramel but without the hassle of making the caramel.

Serves 6   *HIGH 2–3 hours*

Butter, for greasing
½ lime
2 tbsp maple syrup
100g/3½ oz caster sugar
400ml/14 fl oz full fat milk
150ml/¼ pint single cream
5 medium egg yolks
Extra maple syrup, for serving

1. Preheat the slow cooker on High while you prepare the ingredients. Lightly grease and line the base of a deep 18cm/7 inch ovenproof dish with non-stick baking paper. (Check the dish fits inside your slow cooker.)

2. Put the kettle on to boil. Finely grate the lime rind. Swirl the maple syrup over the base of the buttered dish.

3. Pour the sugar, milk and cream into a heavy-based pan and stir in the lime rind. Stirring with a wooden spoon bring almost to the boil (don't let it boil) and remove from the heat.

4. Tip the egg yolks into a bowl and lightly beat. Pour over the hot milk mixture and pour through a fine sieve into the dish. Cover securely with foil.

5. Put the dish into the slow cooker. Pour in sufficient hot water to come half-way up the sides of the dish.

6. Cover with the lid and cook on High for 2–3 hours until firm. Remove from the slow cooker, leave until cold and chill overnight. Loosen the edges and turn onto a plate. Serve cold with extra maple syrup.

Greengages with Coconut

A coconut and Madeira-crumb meringue tops delicious greengages.

Serves 4–6   *HIGH 2–4 hours*

600g/1 lb 5 oz greengages
400g/14 oz Madeira cake
90g/3¼ oz desiccated coconut
3 medium egg whites
100g/3½ oz soft brown sugar
¼ tsp ground nutmeg over top

1. Preheat the slow cooker on High while you prepare the ingredients.

2. Halve and stone the greengages. Finely crumble the Madeira cake.

3. Mix the cake crumbs and coconut in a bowl. In another clean bowl stiffly whisk the egg whites. Slowly whisk in the sugar until it forms soft peaks. Carefully fold into the coconut mix.

4. Arrange the greengages in the base of the slow cooker pot. Pour over 6 tbsp cold water. Cover with the coconut mixture, swirl the surface and sprinkle over the nutmeg.

5. Cover with the lid and cook on High for 2–4 hours until the fruit is tender.

11

COOL CAKES

Cakes from the slow cooker? Can this be for real? Well yes, but these are not exactly the most familiar types of cake. In fact, their flavours and textures are most unusual. These cakes are all moist and sticky; with a dollop of cream or syrup, or some fruit on the side. Most would make excellent puddings.

There's something sophisticated and luxurious about these cakes. They will also be irresistible – some of them will be eaten so rapidly they won't have a chance to go cold. So this is serious temptation. Don't put up any resistance, you're bound to give in.

Extra Chocolaty Chocolate Cake

A treat for all chocolate lovers! For the best flavour use chocolate that contains at least 50 per cent cocoa solids (we like to use 70 per cent). It goes well alongside a cup of strong coffee or as a dessert with thin cream poured over.

Serves 6   *HIGH 1½–2½ hours + 15 minutes*

40g/1½ oz dark chocolate
125g/4½ oz soft butter
125g/4½ oz caster sugar
25g/1 oz ground almonds
2 medium eggs
3 tbsp milk
100g/3½ oz self-raising flour
½ tsp baking powder
25g/1 oz cocoa powder

Icing:
50g/1¾ oz dark chocolate
25g/1 oz butter .
1 tbsp double cream

1. Preheat the slow cooker while you prepare the ingredients and make the cake.

2. Put the kettle on to boil. Butter the inside of an 18–20cm/7–8 inch ovenproof soufflé dish or deep cake tin. Line the base with a circle of non-stick baking paper.

3.   Chop the chocolate into small pieces. Put the butter, caster sugar, almonds, eggs and milk into a large mixing bowl. Sift over the flour, baking powder and cocoa. Beat well for 2–3 minutes until smooth, light and fluffy. Fold in the chocolate pieces.

4.   Spoon the mixture into the prepared dish or tin, roughly levelling the surface.

5.   Put the dish into the slow cooker and pour round sufficient boiling water (from the kettle) to come half-way up its sides.

6.   Cover with the lid and cook on High for 1½–2½ hours until firm to the touch and cooked through.

7.   Meanwhile, prepare the icing ingredients. Break the chocolate into a small ovenproof bowl and add the butter and cream. Cover securely with clear film or foil.

8.   Carefully lift the cake out of the slow cooker and put the bowl of icing ingredients in its place. Replace the lid and cook for about 15 minutes or until the chocolate has melted.

9.   Leave the cake to stand in its dish for 5 minutes before running a knife around the sides if necessary to loosen them, then turning the cake out onto a wire rack lined with a sheet of non-stick baking paper (to prevent the cake sticking to the rack). Leave to cool.

10. As soon as the chocolate has melted, stir the icing ingredients until smooth and glossy. Spread the mixture over the top of the cake and leave to cool completely.

Chocolate Cake with a Nut Topping

Nutty, cocoa and cinnamon cake topped with a squidgy topping.

Serves 6   *HIGH 3–4 hours*

100g/3½ oz butter, plus extra for greasing
60g/2¼ oz shelled, blanched nuts, such as almonds,
  pecan or hazelnuts
3 medium eggs
100g/3½ oz self-raising flour
¼ tsp ground cinnamon
2 tbsp cocoa powder
200g/7 oz light brown caster sugar
Icing sugar, to dust

1. Preheat the slow cooker on High while you prepare the ingredients.

2. Lightly grease and line the base of a deep 18cm/7 inch cake tin with non-stick baking paper. (Check the tin fits inside your slow cooker.) Put the kettle on to boil. Roughly chop the nuts. Take one of the eggs and separate the yolk from the white.

3. Sift the flour, cinnamon and half of the cocoa powder into a large bowl. Add the 2 remaining eggs plus the extra yolk, half the sugar and half the chopped nuts. Beat until well mixed and fluffy. In a clean bowl whisk the egg white until stiff, fold in the remaining sugar and whisk until soft. Stir in the remaining cocoa powder and nuts.

4. Spoon the cake mixture into the prepared tin and swirl the meringue mixture on top.

5. Put the tin into the slow cooker. Pour in sufficient hot water to come half-way up the sides of the tin. Cover with the lid and cook on High for 3–4 hours.

6. Lift the tin out of the slow cooker and leave to stand for 15 minutes. Loosen the edges with a knife and carefully turn out. (It doesn't matter if the surface breaks.) Leave to cool, dust thickly with icing sugar and cut into wedges.

Cardamom & Ginger Cake with Sesame & Pine Nuts

You might be more familiar with the use of cardamom in savoury dishes, but it adds a lovely favour to cakes and biscuits as well. Here we've teamed it with the peppery sweet flavour of ginger and added sesame seeds and pine nuts for crunch.

Serves 8   *HIGH 3–4 hours*

100g/3½ oz butter, plus extra for greasing
100g/3½ oz wholemeal self-raising flour
½ tsp baking powder
½ tsp ground cardamom
1 tsp ground ginger
100g/3½ oz light brown caster sugar
2 medium eggs
1 tsp vanilla extract
1 tbsp clear honey
60g/2¼ oz sesame seeds
2 tbsp pine nuts
Icing sugar, to dust

1.   Preheat the slow cooker on High while you prepare the ingredients.

2.   Lightly grease and line the base of a deep 18cm/7 inch cake tin with non-stick baking paper. (Check the tin fits inside your slow cooker.) Put the kettle on to boil.

3. Sift the flour, baking powder, cardamom and ginger into a large bowl. Cut the butter into small cubes and add to the flour mixture. Using your fingertips, rub the butter into the flour and spices until the mixture resembles fine crumbs (or do this part in a food processor). Add the sugar, eggs, vanilla, honey and sesame seeds. Beat until well mixed, soft and smooth.

4. Spoon into the prepared tin, smooth the surface and scatter the pine nuts over the top.

5. Put the tin into the slow cooker. Pour in sufficient hot water to come half-way up the sides of the tin. Cover with the lid and cook on High for 3–4 hours.

6. Lift the tin out of the slow cooker and leave to stand for 5 minutes. Loosen the edges with a knife and turn out. Leave to cool, dust with icing sugar and cut into wedges.

Sticky Oat, Orange & Walnut Cake

Lovely – a sticky, nutty, orange-flavoured cake made with oats for flavour and texture.

Serves 6–8   HIGH 3–4 hours

100g/3½ oz butter, plus extra for greasing
1 small orange
60g/2¼ oz walnut pieces
60g/2¼ oz golden syrup
60g/2¼ oz light brown sugar
100g/3½ oz rolled oats
60g/2¼ oz self-raising flour
2 medium eggs

1. Preheat the slow cooker on High while you prepare the ingredients.

2. Lightly grease and line the base of a deep 18cm/7 inch ovenproof dish with non-stick baking paper. (Check the dish fits inside your slow cooker.) Put the kettle on to boil. Finely grate the rind from half the orange. Cut the orange in half and squeeze out the juice. Roughly chop the walnuts.

3. Put the butter, syrup and sugar into a small pan. Gently heat, stirring continuously until melted. Remove from the heat and pour into a large bowl. Stir in the oats, flour, orange rind and juice, then add the eggs (the mixture mustn't be too hot). Mix thoroughly and spoon into the prepared dish.

4. Cover the dish tightly with foil and put into the slow cooker. Pour in sufficient hot water to come half-way up the sides of the dish. Cover with the lid and cook on High for 3–4 hours.

5. Lift the dish out of the slow cooker and leave to stand for 5 minutes. Loosen the edges with a knife and turn out. Leave to cool and cut into wedges.

Sticky Pineapple & Cinnamon Cake

Good just as it is, with a cup of tea or coffee, or cut into wedges and served with a generous spoonful of crème fraîche for dessert.

Serves 6   *HIGH 1½–2½ hours*

125g/4½ oz butter, plus extra for greasing
125g/4½ oz crystallised pineapple
2 medium eggs
125g/4½ oz self-raising flour
1½ tsp ground cinnamon
175g/6 oz golden syrup
125g/4½ oz soft light brown sugar
Icing sugar

1. Preheat the slow cooker while you prepare the ingredients and make the cake.

2. Put the kettle on to boil. Butter the inside of an 18–20cm/7–8 inch ovenproof soufflé dish or deep cake tin. Line the base with a circle of non-stick baking paper.

3. Chop the pineapple into small pieces. Lightly beat the eggs. Sift the flour with the cinnamon. With the fingertips, rub the butter into the flour until the mixture resembles fine breadcrumbs (alternatively you could do this in a food processor). Add the golden syrup, sugar and eggs and beat until smooth. Stir in the pineapple.

4. Spoon the mixture into the prepared dish or tin, roughly levelling the surface.

5. Put the dish into the slow cooker and pour round sufficient boiling water (from the kettle) to come half-way up its sides.

6. Cover with the lid and cook on High for 1½–2½ hours until firm to the touch and cooked through.

7. Carefully lift the dish out of the slow cooker and leave the cake to stand for 5 minutes. Run a knife around the sides to loosen them, then turn the cake out onto a wire rack lined with a sheet of non-stick baking paper (to prevent the cake sticking to the rack). Leave to cool completely.

8. Just before serving, sift a little icing sugar over the top.

Lemon Drizzle Polenta Cake

You'll find this cake irresistible.

Serves 6   *HIGH 2½–3 hours*

125g/4½ oz soft butter, plus extra for greasing
2 medium eggs
2 lemons
100g/3½ oz caster sugar
100g/3½ oz self-raising flour
125g/4½ oz polenta (cornmeal)
125g/4½ oz icing sugar

1. Preheat the slow cooker while you prepare the ingredients and make the cake.

2. Put the kettle on to boil. Butter the inside of an 18–20cm/7–8 inch ovenproof soufflé dish or deep cake tin. Line the base with a circle of non-stick baking paper.

3. Lightly beat the eggs. Finely grate the rind from one lemon and squeeze the juice from two (you will need about 7 tbsp lemon juice).

4. Beat the butter with the sugar until light and fluffy. Gradually beat in the eggs. Sift the flour over the top and add the polenta and 4 tbsp lemon juice. Using a large metal spoon, fold in, until the mixture is smooth.

5. Spoon the mixture into the prepared dish or tin, roughly levelling the surface. Put the dish into the slow cooker and pour round sufficient boiling water (from the kettle) to come half-way up its sides.

6. Cover with the lid and cook on High for 2½–3 hours until firm to the touch and cooked through.

7. Meanwhile, make the drizzle mixture by blending the remaining 3 tbsp lemon juice with the icing sugar until smooth.

8. Carefully lift the dish out of the slow cooker and leave the cake to stand for 5 minutes. Run a knife around the sides to loosen them, then turn the cake out onto a wire rack lined with a sheet of non-stick baking paper (to prevent the cake sticking to the rack). Using a fine skewer, make several holes in the top of the warm cake and slowly spoon the drizzle over the top. Leave to cool before serving.

12

TOP PRESERVES

You always need preserves at the ready. We don't know where we would be without our home-made supply of preserves, and a great way to make these is to use your slow cooker.

Curds, butters, conserves, relishes, chutneys and sauces – all of them can be created in a slow cooker. They will then be at hand to serve (as spreads, fillings, toppings or accompaniments) with toast, pancakes or ice cream, with cheeses and with cold meats, or in a host of other ways. And just think of all those recipes containing instructions to spread, drizzle or spoon preserves onto the mixture for cooking or onto the finished dish.

Preserves can be stored quite happily in the fridge. They won't be there long, though, because they are so useful and so appetising you will soon need to make some more.

Date & Apricot Relish

A sticky sweet relish which can be spooned onto pancakes or ice cream or served with cold ham or smoked mackerel. Store in the refrigerator and use within three months.

Makes about 1.3kg/3 lb   *LOW 4–6 hours*

1 unwaxed lemon
350g/12 oz dried pitted dates
350g/12 oz dried apricots
2 green apples
250g/9 oz granulated sugar
400ml/14 fl oz unsweetened apple juice
25g/1 oz butter
1 tsp ground allspice

1. Preheat the slow cooker on High while you prepare the ingredients.

2. Finely grate the rind from the lemon, cut in half and squeeze the juice. Finely chop the dates and apricots. Cut the apples into quarters, remove the cores and cut the fruit into small pieces (no need to peel them).

3. Put all the ingredients into the slow cooker and stir well.

4. Cover with the lid and cook on Low for 4–6 hours, stirring occasionally after the first 2 hours until cooked and thickened.

5. Stir well before spooning into warm sterilised jars and sealing.

Autumn Fruit Spread

Though this preserve is cooked over two days, it requires only a little attention from the cook and is ideal for using up windfalls. The skins are left on the fruit to give the best possible flavour to the finished fruit butter. Spread it on hot toast or use it to sandwich cakes or meringues. Store in the refrigerator and use within 4 weeks.

Makes about 900g/2 lb   LOW 8–10 hours + HIGH 5–8 hours

1kg/2½ lb cooking apples
1kg/2¼ lb firm pears
1 lemon
225g/8 oz golden caster sugar
½ tsp ground cinnamon
250ml/9 fl oz apple juice

1. Cut the apples and pears into quarters, remove their stalks and cores (leave their skins in place) and chop into small pieces. Finely grate the rind from the lemon and squeeze out its juice.

2. Toss the chopped fruit with the lemon rind and juice, sugar and cinnamon. Tip the mixture into the slow cooker, pressing it down gently to make an even layer. Pour the apple juice over the top.

3. Cover with the lid and cook on Low for 8–10 hours or overnight until the fruit is very soft.

4. Mash and stir the fruit well.

5. Switch the slow cooker to High and continue cooking, uncovered, for a further 5–8 hours or until the mixture is very thick.

6. Press the mixture through a sieve and discard the skins. Spoon the fruit purée into warmed, sterilised jars and seal.

Apple, Plum & Walnut Chutney

The long, gentle cooking creates wonderfully mature flavours in this chutney. You will want to start eating it as soon as it has cooled – try it with cheeses and cold meats or spooned into a bacon sandwich. It is best kept in the refrigerator and used within 2 months.

Makes about 1.25kg/2¾ lb   *HIGH 5–8 hours*

675g/1½ lb cooking apples
250g/9 oz firm red plums
2 medium onions
2 garlic cloves
1 small red chilli (see page 15)
200g/7 oz walnut pieces
150ml/¼ pint red or white wine vinegar
450g/1 lb soft light brown sugar
1 tsp mixed spice
1 tsp ground ginger

1. Preheat the slow cooker on High while you prepare the ingredients.

2. Cut the apples into quarters and remove their cores and chop (no need to peel them). Halve the plums, remove their stones and chop. Finely chop the onions and garlic. Remove the stalk and seed from the chilli, and slice thinly. Roughly chop the walnuts.

3. Put all the ingredients into the slow cooker and mix well before levelling the surface.

4. Cover with the lid and cook on High for 5–8 hours, stirring occasionally, until very soft and thick.

5. Spoon into warmed, sterilised jars and seal.

Red Pepper Chutney

It won't be as sweet but try this recipe with green, orange or yellow peppers. Keep refrigerated and use within 6–8 weeks.

Makes about 1.6kg/3½ lb   *LOW 4–6 hours*

1 kg/2¼ lb red peppers
2 red chillies (see page 15)
3 green apples
2 medium red onions
2 garlic cloves
200g/7 oz sultanas
300ml/½ pint vinegar, cider or red wine
225g/8 oz soft brown sugar
2 tsp fennel seeds
1 tsp ground cloves
1 tsp salt
1 tsp ground black pepper

1.   Preheat the slow cooker on High while you prepare the ingredients.

2.   Cut the peppers and chillies in half, remove and discard the seeds and stalks, and finely chop. Cut the apples into quarters, remove the cores and cut the fruit into small pieces (no need to peel them). Finely chop the onions and the garlic.

3.   Tip the chopped fruits and vegetables into the slow cooker and stir in the remaining ingredients.

4.   Cover with the lid and cook on Low for 4–6 hours, stirring twice, until thick.

5.   Stir well before spooning into warm sterilised jars and sealing.

Citrus Curd

*There is nothing to beat the citrusy tang of home-made curd.
It makes a lovely filling for cakes or meringues, as well as for
spreading on fresh bread or hot toast. Use unwaxed fruits if
possible. The curd should be stored in the refrigerator and
used within 4 weeks – that's if you can resist it!*

Makes about 1kg/2¼ lb   *LOW 3–4 hours*

2 large lemons
1 lime
1 small orange
125g/4½ oz unsalted butter
450g/1 lb caster sugar
4 medium eggs

1. Scrub and dry the fruit. Finely grate the rind from the
    lemons, lime and orange, and squeeze out their juice.
    Cut the butter into small pieces.

2. Put the citrus rinds and juice into a pan on the hob and
    add the butter and sugar. Heat gently, stirring, until the
    butter has melted and the sugar has dissolved. Leave to
    cool.

3. Meanwhile, preheat the slow cooker on High. Put the
    kettle on to boil.

4. Beat the eggs and stir them into the cooled mixture. Strain into a 1.2 litre/2 pint pudding bowl (straining removes any stringy pieces of egg white).

5. Cover with a sheet of non-stick paper and then a sheet of foil. Scrunch the edges tightly to the sides of the dish, securing them well.

6. Stand the dish in the slow cooker and pour round sufficient boiling water (from the kettle) to come half-way up its sides.

7. Cover with the lid and cook on Low for 3–4 hours, stirring once or twice after the first 1½ hours if possible, until the curd has thickened.

8. Pour into warmed, sterilised jars and seal.

Chilli Chocolate Sauce

Rich, dark, spicy Mexican sauces are used to add a smooth, rich flavour to meat and poultry dishes. The combination of chocolate and chilli may be a surprise but they do complement each other. Be bold: try a little with plain sorbet. Keep in the refrigerator and use within 2–3 weeks.

Makes about 1.25kg/2¾ lb   HIGH 2½–3 hours + 30 minutes

500g/1 lb 2 oz piece of squash or pumpkin
200g/7 oz dried apricots
Small piece of fresh root ginger
3 red chillies (see page 15)
225g/8 oz plain dark chocolate
500ml/18 fl oz unsweetened apple juice
140g/5 oz sesame seeds

1. Preheat the slow cooker on High while you prepare the ingredients.

2. With a spoon, scoop out the seeds from the squash or pumpkin. Cut away the thick peel and chop the flesh into even-sized pieces. Quarter the apricots. With a small, sharp knife scrape the skin from the root ginger and finely grate. Cut the chillies in half, remove and discard the seeds and stalks, and finely chop. Coarsely grate the chocolate and reserve until later.

3. Tip the squash or pumpkin into the slow cooker and add the apricots, ginger and chillies. Pour over the apple juice and stir well.

4. Cover with the lid and cook on High for 2½–3 hours stirring once.

5. Stir in the sesame seeds, re-cover and cook for a further 30 minutes.

6. Remove the lid and use a stick blender to whizz the sauce smooth.

7. Scatter over the grated chocolate and stir until melted. The sauce should be quite thick.

8. Stir well before spooning into warm sterilised jars and sealing.

13

CLEVER EXTRAS

There's many a meal that can be enhanced by the addition of some well-judged, last-minute extras. Extras can provide added textures, crunch or bite, or fresh, contrasting flavours and colour to complement the pleasures of the principal dish. And you might, of course, want to make a dish go further; if so, pastry, scones or garlic bread add substance to your main meal and can set it off a treat.

There are good things here to stir in, like the pesto or curry paste, or to sprinkle over, like the crushed crisps, nachos or tortillas, or to fold in, like the rice noodles, or to serve alongside, like the stir-fried or steamed vegetables

All these clever extras can give a final flourish to a meal as it makes its way to the table.

Last-minute additions can freshen up a dish by adding crunch, a complementary flavour or a pastry, bread or scone topping. All are added towards, or at, the end of the cooking time. We've given both sweet and savoury suggestions.

Pastry
Ready-made pastry makes it easy to transform dishes into pies. Lift the cooked dish in its pottery liner out of the slow cooker and top with a sheet of short-crust or flaky pastry or buttered sheets of filo pastry and bake in a hot oven until risen and golden. Or pre-cook discs or shapes of pastry and put a couple on top of each serving.

Scones
In place of pastry, try sweet or savoury scones. Use a basic recipe and flavour with chopped fresh herbs, such as rosemary, parsley or oregano, cheese and mustard or nuts, lemon rind, ground ginger or cinnamon.

Parcels
Fish or shellfish can be wrapped in a foil parcel and put on top of vegetables cooking in the slow cooker.

Concentrated Sauces
Add extra flavour with a spoonful or two of red or green pesto, horseradish cream, mint jelly, cranberry sauce or tapenade.

Noodles
Rice noodles only need soaking in cold water; drained and added towards the end of the cooking time, they give a complete meal in one pot.

Crunchy Things
Plain or flavoured crisps, nachos, tortilla chips, biscuits, meringues, brandy snaps or ice cream cornets can be lightly crushed and scattered over the dish.

Breads
Toasted breads made from thinly sliced bagels, sweet brioche, wedges of flour tortillas, mini nan breads flavoured with garlic, tomato or cheese make a tasty topping to bean, meat, fish or fruit dishes.

Drop in some Dumplings
Add dumplings to your favourite stews during the final stages of cooking. Simply sift 100g/3½ oz self-raising flour with 1 tsp baking powder and a little seasoning, and stir in 50g/1¾ oz shredded suet. Mix in sufficient cold water to make a soft dough and drop balls of the mixture on top of the stew, cover and continue cooking for 30–40 minutes.

Roasted and Toasted
Oven-roasted or pan-fried fruits and vegetables such as onion rings, pepper slices, apple wedges and orange slices add another dimension. Toasted breadcrumbs, nuts and coconut all give added crunch.

Added Bite
Stir-fried or steamed vegetables will add colour and 'bite'.

Fresh Herbs
Adding fresh herbs just before serving will intensify the flavours.

Gremolata and Salsas
A spoonful of finely chopped fresh herbs, garlic and lemon rind adds extra zest. Or include tomatoes, chilli and a little oil for a real zing.

Finish with a Swirl
Flavour single or double cream, natural yogurt, crème fraîche or smooth tofu with fresh herbs, spices, finely chopped nuts, grated citrus rind, fruit purées, syrups or a little alcohol.

Mayonnaise
Stir crushed garlic, tomato purée, wholegrain mustard or chopped fresh herbs into mayonnaise. Add a small amount to finished dishes.

Sifted Things
For a speedy decoration, sift icing sugar, cocoa powder and drinking chocolate over desserts. Demerara sugar adds crunch and can be browned under a hot grill.

Praline
Delicious with desserts, praline is sugar dissolved in water and boiled until golden and then set hard. You could use crushed peanut brittle.

INDEX

A

Adapting conventional recipes, 13

Apple, Plum & Walnut Chutney, 190

Apples, Pecan-Filled, 154

Aubergines, Potatoes & Carrots with Lemon Myrtle, 117

Autumn Fruit Spread, 189

B

Bagna Cauda, 80

Baked Beans with Pork, Traditional, 62

Barley Pilaff with Lamb & Mushrooms, 130

Beans, dried, 14

Beans with Pork, Traditional Baked, 62

Beef & Chorizo, Chilli, 147

Beef & Pork Meat Loaf, 54

Beef with Red Wine, Garlic & Thyme, 56

Beetroots & Red Cabbage with Tofu, Spiced, 104

Biryani, 138

Borlotti Bean Soup with Spicy Sausage, 38

Breads, 198

Breakfast Fruit, 19

Brioche, Banana & Cranberry Pudding, 156

Browning meat, 14

Butterscotch Pudding, Sticky, 166

C

Cake, Extra Chocolaty Chocolate, 174

Cake, Lemon Drizzle Polenta, 184

Cake, Sticky Oat, Orange & Walnut, 180

Cake, Sticky Pineapple & Cinnamon, 182

Cake with a Nut Topping, Chocolate, 176

Cake with Sesame & Pine Nuts, Cardamom & Ginger, 178

Cardamom & Ginger Cake with Sesame & Pine Nuts, 178

Cassoulet, Quorn, 108

Cheese Fondue with Crispy Bacon, Two-, 70

Chicken & Prawns, 68

Chicken & Vegetable Curry, Thai Green, 142

Chicken Bowl, Chilli, 144

Chicken Chowder, 36

Chicken Dhal, 146

Chicken, Honeyed, 48

Chicken, "Hunter's", 50

Chicken with Egg Noodles, Oriental, 122

Chicken with Whisky & Wild Mushrooms, Mustard, 98

Chickpeas with Cumin, Green Chillies & Parsley, 140

Chilli Beef & Chorizo, 147

Chilli Brown Rice with Prawns & Seeds, 125

Chilli Chicken Bowl, 144

Chilli Chocolate Sauce, 194
Chilli Venison with Chocolate, 81
Chilli with Pan-Fried Tofu, Vegetable, 106
Chillies, 15
Chinese Pork with Cashews, 150
Chocolate & Lime Pancakes, 20
Chocolate & Rum Fondue, 164
Chocolate Cake, Extra Chocolaty, 174
Chocolate Cake with a Nut Topping, 176
Chocolate Ginger Pudding, 158
Chocolate Rice Pudding, 170
Chocolate Sauce, Chilli, 194
Chutney, Apple, Plum & Walnut, 190
Chutney, Red Pepper, 191
Citrus Curd, 192
Cooking times, 13
Courgette & Mushroom Frittata, 26
Cream, 199
Creamy Squash & Sweet Potato Casserole, 114
Crumble, Plums & Berry, 155
Curd, Citrus, 192
Curried Turkey & Sweet Potato Layer, 52
Curry, Thai Green & Vegetable, 142
Curry with Coconut, Mild Lamb, 152

D
Date & Apricot Relish, 188
Devilled Frankfurters, Gammon & Smoked Sausage, 28
Dhal, Chicken, 146
Dhal, Tarka, 136
Dried beans, soaking, 14
Duck with Pomegranate Juice, 90
Dumplings, 198

E
Egg Custard with Lime & Maple Syrup, 171
Eggs, 15

F
Fennel & Red Pepper Soup with Tamarind & Mint, 43
Figs with Orange, Honey & Walnuts, Warm, 23
Fish, 198
Flageolet & Black-Eyed Beans with Pistou, 100
Fondue, Chocolate & Rum, 164
Fondue with Crispy Bacon, Two-Cheese, 70
Food, quantity of, 13
Frankfurters, Gammon & Smoked Sausage, Devilled, 28
Fruit, Breakfast, 19
Fruit Pudding, Tropical, 160
Fruit Spread, Autumn, 189

G
Game Terrine, 76
Gammon, Slow-Cooked, 66
Ginger, Cake with Sesame & Pine Nuts, Cardamom &, 178
Ginger Pudding, Chocolate, 158
Green Lentil & Apple Soup, 144
Greengages with Coconut, 172
Gremolata, 199

H
Haddock, Rice with Smoked, 24
Ham Salad, Hot Cracked Wheat &, 132
Honeyed Chicken, 48
Hot Cracked Wheat & Ham Salad, 132
Hot Muesli with Cranberries & Blueberries, 22
"Hunter's" Chicken, 50

L
Lamb Chops on Caramelised Squash, 92
Lamb Couscous, 128
Lamb Curry with Coconut, Mild, 152
Lamb Meatballs in Tomato Sauce, 60
Lamb Shanks, Lancashire, 94

Lamb with Apricots, Spiced, 148
Lamb with Onion & Courgette
    Sauce, Stuffed Shoulder of,
    74
Lamb with Red Wine & Lentils, 58
Lancashire Lamb Shanks, 94
Leeks, Bacon & Cheese, Brown
    Rice with, 126
Leg of Lamb with Red Wine &
    Lentils, 58
Leg of Pork Cooked in Cider,
    Spiced, 72
Lemon Drizzle Polenta Cake, 184
Lentils, Root Vegetables, Star
    Anise & Lemon, 116
Lid, lifting the, 14

M
Marrow with Bulgur Wheat,
    Pepper & Ginger Stuffing,
    112
Mayonnaise, 199
Meat, browning, 14
Meatballs in Tomato Sauce,
    Lamb, 60
Mild Lamb Curry with Coconut,
    152
Minestrone Stew, 110
Muesli with Cranberries &
    Blueberries, Hot, 22
Mushroom & Parmesan Rice, 124
Mustard Chicken with Whisky &
    Wild Mushrooms, 98

N
Noodles, rice, 198

O
Oriental Chicken with Egg
    Noodles, 122

P
Pancakes, Chocolate & Lime, 20
Pasta, Mushroom & Bean
    Medley, 120
Pasta, Trout & Fennel, 121
Pastry, 197

Pecan-Filled Apples, 154
Peppers with Spiced Cheese
    Stuffing, 88
Pheasant in Orange & Apple
    Sauce, 96
Pilaff with Lamb & Mushrooms,
    Barley, 130
Plum Pudding, 168
Plums & Berry Crumble, 155
Pork Cooked in Cider, Spiced
    Leg of, 72
Pork Meat Loaf, Beef &, 54
Pork, Sweet & Sour, 64
Pork with Cashews, Chinese, 150
Porridge, Weekend, 18
Potato, Leek & Smoked Ham
    Soup with Olives, 42
Praline, 199
Preheating the slow cooker, 15
Pudding, Brioche, Banana &
    Cranberry, 156
Pudding, Chocolate Ginger, 158
Pudding, Chocolate Rice, 170
Pudding, Plum, 168
Pudding, Squash & Raisin, 162
Pudding, Sticky Butterscotch, 166
Pudding, Tropical Fruit, 160

Q
Quorn Cassoulet, 108

R
Red Pepper Chutney, 191
Relish, Date & Apricot, 188
Rice, 14
Rice, Mushroom & Parmesan,
    124
Rice noodles, 198
Rice Pudding, Chocolate, 170
Rice with Chicken, Mussels &
    Prawns, Spanish-Style, 78
Rice with Leeks, Bacon &
    Cheese, Brown, 126
Rice with Prawns & Seeds, Chilli
    Brown, 125
Rice with Smoked Haddock, 24
Root Vegetables & Red Beans in
    Spiced Coconut Sauce, 102

S

Salad, Hot Cracked Wheat & Ham, 132
Salad, Warm Millet, 134
Salmon & Prawns with Vermouth, 86
Salsa, 199
Sauce, Chilli Chocolate, 194
Sauces, 198
Scones, 197
Seafood in a Wine & Herb Soup, 84
Shellfish, 198
Shoulder of Lamb with Onion & Courgette Sauce, Stuffed, 74
Slow-Cooked Gammon, 66
Soups, 31 *et seq.*
Spanish-Style Rice with Chicken, Mussels & Prawns, 78
Spiced Beetroots & Red Cabbage with Tofu, 104
Spiced Lamb with Apricots, 148
Spiced Leg of Pork Cooked in Cider, 72
Spoon measures, 15
Spread, Autumn Fruit, 189
Squash & Raisin Pudding, 162
Squash & Sweet Potato Casserole, Creamy, 114
Stew, Minestrone, 110
Sticky Butterscotch Pudding, 166
Sticky Oat, Orange & Walnut Cake, 180
Sticky Pineapple & Cinnamon Cake, 182
Stuffed Shoulder of Lamb with Onion & Courgette Sauce, 74

Sweet & Sour Pork, 64
Sweet Potato & Chickpea Soup, 34
Sweet Potato Casserole, Creamy Squash &, 114

T

Tarka Dhal, 136
Terrine, Game, 76
Thai Curry Soup with Pork, Chilli & Lemon Grass, 40
Thai Green Chicken & Vegetable Curry, 142
Tomato, Basil & Rice Soup, 32
Traditional Baked Beans with Pork, 62
Tropical Fruit Pudding, 160
Trout & Fennel Pasta, 121
Turkey & Sweet Potato Layer, Curried, 52
Two-Cheese Fondue with Crispy Bacon, 70

V

Vegetable Chilli with Pan-Fried Tofu, 106
Vegetables, 14, 198
Vegetables, browning, 14
Venison with Chocolate, Chilli, 81

W

Walnut Cake, Sticky Oat, Orange &, 180
Warm Figs with Orange, Honey & Walnuts, 23
Warm Millet Salad, 132
Weekend Porridge, 18

Also in the Right Way series

SLOW COOKING PROPERLY EXPLAINED

by Dianne Page

Dianne Page's collection of over 100 traditional family recipes for the slow cooker has been a bestseller for thirty years. Updated frequently to cover the latest developments in slow cooking, her recipes prove that slow cookers not only produce tasty soups, stews and casseroles but are also ideal for cooking fish, fruit and vegetables.

The benefits of slow cooking are:

● Flavours have time to blend and develop

● Tenderizes even the toughest cheapest meats – with succulent results

● Uses far less energy than a conventional oven

● Offers flexible meal times for busy families

● Produces no cooking smells and steam in the kitchen

The book also includes a guide to help you choose a slow cooker that suits your needs, plus tips on how to adapt your own recipes for slow cooking.

FRESH BREAD IN THE MORNING
FROM YOUR BREAD MACHINE

by Annette Yates

Wake up to the aroma of fresh bread wafting through your kitchen every morning! A dream? No. With your bread machine, it's a reality. Push a button or two and transform what seems like a laborious, time-consuming and skilled process into a spectacularly easy affair.

So why do you need a book when bread machines come with their own recipes? Well, such recipes vary, sometimes on the high side, in the amount of yeast, salt, sugar, fat and dried milk powder they contain. Annette Yates has set about reducing these ingredients and providing recipes for making loaves that are as natural as possible. And they are delicious too.

Or you can add extra ingredients – like herbs, spices, seeds, nuts, fruit, vegetables, honey, mustard and even chocolate! – to transform simple bread into something special. Try it and see . . .

THE CURRY SECRET

by Kris Dhillon

This is the curry book with a difference! It gives the secret of *Indian Restaurant Cooking* – not the traditional cuisine practised by Indians at home but the particularly interesting and distinctive variety that is served in Indian restaurants worldwide.

Kris Dhillon writes with the authority of an accomplished Indian restaurateur, with many years' experience and thousands of satisfied customers. Most chefs guard closely the secret of their basic curry sauce, but here Kris Dhillon reveals all, and offers you the opportunity to reproduce chicken, lamb, fish and vegetable curries with that elusive taste.

Three ways to order *Right Way* books:

1. Visit www.constablerobinson.com and order through our website.

2. Telephone the TBS order line on 01206 255 800.
    Order lines are open Monday – Friday, 8:30am – 5:30pm.

3. Use this order form and send a cheque made payable to TBS Ltd
    or charge my [ ] Visa [ ] Mastercard [ ] Maestro (issue
    no_____)

Card number: _____

Expiry date: _____ Last three digits on back of card: _____

Signature: _____

(your signature is essential when paying by credit or debit card)

No. of copies	Title	Price	Total
	Slow Cooking Properly Explained	£5.99	
	Fresh Bread in the Morning	£5.99	
	The Curry Secret	£5.99	
	For P&P add £2.75 for the first book, 60p for each additional book		
	Grand Total		£

Name: _____

Address: _____

_____ Postcode: _____

Daytime Tel. No./Email
(in case of query)   _____

**Please return forms to Cash Sales/Direct Mail Dept., The Book
Service, Colchester Road, Frating Green, Colchester CO7 7DW.**

Enquiries to readers@constablerobinson.com.

Constable and Robinson Ltd (directly or via its agents) may mail, email
or phone you about promotions or products.

[ ] Tick box if you do not want these from us [ ] or our subsidiaries.

www.constablerobinson.com